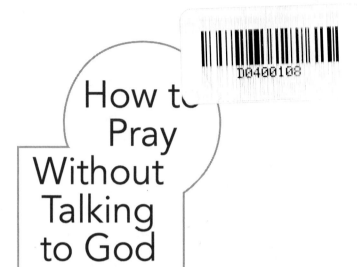

How to Pray Without Talking to God

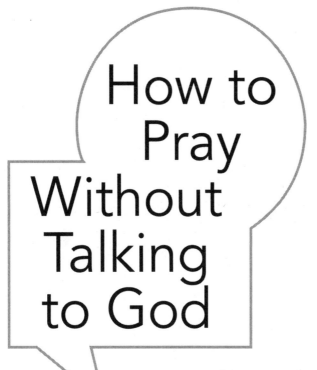

How to Pray Without Talking to God

moment by moment,
choice by choice

LINDA MARTELLA-WHITSETT

Best Spiritual Author Competition Winner

HAMPTON ROADS

Cover design: Jim Warner

Cover art: Henry De Lattre's Cazique (Delattria Henrica), 1861, by John Gould. Academy of Natural Sciences, Philadelphia. Copyright © Academy of Natural Sciences/SuperStock.

Author photo: Janne Aubrey

Interior design: Dutton & Sherman

Hampton Roads Publishing Company, Inc.
Charlottesville, VA 22906
Distributed by Red Wheel/Weiser, LLC
www.redwheelweiser.com

Library of Congress Cataloging-in-Publication Data is available upon request.

ISBN: 978-1-57174-668-9

MAL

10 9 8 7 6 5

Printed on acid-free paper in the United States of America

Contents

Beloved reader,

My deepest desire is to expand our awareness of All That Is—one of my favorite names for GOD. Chances are you have a favorite name for GOD. Chances are you have opened this book because your awareness of GOD has expanded beyond religious conventions. Perhaps you, like countless others, are leaving your church, temple, synagogue, or mosque in disillusionment. Maybe you are filled with knowledge based upon your religion's teachings about GOD, all the while longing to *experience* GOD. Maybe you are ready for a concept of GOD that is unconfined by dogma and an experience of GOD that is intimate as well as expansive.

My deepest desire is for each of us to realize all that GOD is, we are. Although to some readers this may appear an outrageous, even blasphemous, assertion, to me it is the key to affirmative prayer. GOD cannot be diminished when a person asserts her Divine Identity. To the contrary, GOD appears bigger, brighter, and more glorious when we bring into visibility the invisible GOD. The importance of Jesus Christ, the prophet Muhammad (peace be upon him), and spiritual masters of all ages does not diminish by an individual's assertion of his Divine Identity. Rather, we honor them for their achievement of GOD-consciousness, and we accept their guidance about how we too might live as visible evidence of the invisible GOD.

As you read this book, I uphold your highest intentions. I celebrate your Divine Identity. I appreciate your deepening realization of Divine Power revealed in prayer. You and I have no greater work to do in the world today than to pray. May our wonderful world benefit from our rising divine consciousness.

—Linda Martella-Whitsett

Chapter 1

Know Your Divine Identity

Do you not know that you are God's temple and that God's Spirit dwells in you? . . . For God's temple is holy, and that temple you are.

—1 Corinthians 3:16–17*

Words and methods of praying are informed by our understanding of Divine Nature. Understand Divine Nature and your Divine Identity.

God Is Not a Superhuman

Sitting on a deck above the Guadalupe River, I was enjoying the gurgle of the water below and the intermittent chatter of the wildlife around me. I felt centered on that spiritual renewal retreat, content on my third evening away from the demands of daily living. Then a deep human voice intruded from

---

* All Bible quotations come from the New Revised Standard Version.

the porch next door. My neighbor was speaking to someone on the telephone, becoming louder by the minute. He said something about God. I listened. Next thing I heard: "I've been praying about your diabetes for two weeks. It's gonna work. I know it. God's gonna take care of it."

Having been a student and a teacher in a New Thought denomination, I was surprised that I felt surprised by this well-intentioned man's statement. But I knew my way of understanding the Divine Nature and my way of praying could be seen as blasphemous to this kind man. I believed—and continue to believe—the Divine Nature is not a person who cares how people pray. In fact, prayer researcher Dr. Larry Dossey confirmed in experiments that any form of heartfelt praying makes a difference. Yet, it mattered to me that my neighbor seemed to be gambling regarding his friend's health—blowing breath into his hands holding the dice, saying *This time it's gonna work. I know it.*

I blessed that other person, the person on the other end of the telephone line, and the situation. I was cool. And then I went to a gathering of colleagues, or maybe I listened to another New Thought church's podcast—I can't remember exactly what I did next. But I do remember what I thought: I was surprised again to hear people who had studied what I had studied saying *Dear God, thank you for this; help us with that.* I wanted to shout, "Stop talking to God! GOD is not a superhuman!"

Little children, concrete thinkers that they are, believe what they see. They see someone in a Santa Claus costume as proof of Santa Claus's existence. When my son, Adrian, was two and a half, a neighbor came to our house in a Santa suit one evening after Adrian had gone to sleep. I went into my son's room to rouse him just as Santa was walking up the stairs, jingling all the way. Before Adrian saw Santa, he heard the bells. From that night until age twelve, much later than most other children, Adrian knew Santa was real because he had heard sleigh bells.

In the years after Adrian recovered from disillusionment about Santa, he found a new delight in the holiday season. He realized the spirit of Santa Claus is the spirit of giving, loving, and caring. He could embody the Santa spirit even though he no longer believed that mythical man actually existed.

Eventually everyone realizes that Santa Claus is not a superhuman. GOD is not a superhuman either.

Evolve Your God

Sooner or later, every child must grow up. Everyone must become self-sufficient. Those who do not mature live out their lives handicapped by dependency. Sooner or later, I believe, everyone must evolve in spiritual understanding and claim divine self-sufficiency. All spiritual masters have done so, even as they credit the One Power that is inclusive of their humanity as well as greater than it. Those who do not mature spiritually feel powerless and dependent upon a divine parent they must plead with and please.

Come along with me, and I will share with you my evolving understanding of Divine Nature. While I describe my experience, I invite you to tune in to your own unfolding understanding.

As we begin, notice two variations of the printed word *God*. Throughout the book, *God* is used in quotations as well as when the Divine is personified. GOD is used to highlight an understanding of the Divine as All That Is, not a person but a power.

The Invisible Parent

For many years, I believed in a God I had to plead with and please. From early childhood through my teens, I thought of God as physically "out there," as an unseen parent, and specifically as an unseen male parent. I could ask God for help but never could hear him talk to me; God could see me, but I could not see him. God was an elusive superparent, far away from me but watching me and holding all the cards.

Bible stories from my childhood reinforced this notion. God was, I learned, the *cause* of all human experience, especially human suffering. Everyone I knew believed in the God who would not show himself to us and caused car accidents, diseases, and death. God had all the control and wielded it, like the Wizard of Oz, from behind a curtain.

While God was unseen, he was demanding. Under threat of eternal damnation, he required my attendance at Sunday Mass, my abstinence from meat on Fridays, and my admission of sins to a priest. God would reward me when I behaved well. God would punish me when I misbehaved. "He sees you when you're sleeping. He knows when you're awake. He knows if you've been bad or good, so be good for goodness' sake" might have been sung about God as well as Santa.

The threat of God's punishment was so instilled in me that I imagined the religious statues in my childhood home had eyes—especially the Blessed Mother statue on my bedroom windowsill. Oh yes! When in adolescence I was discovering the pleasurable feelings of my pubescent body, I turned the Blessed Mother statue around so she would not be able to watch me.

The Bodyguard

"And He walks with me and He talks with me and He tells me I am His own . . ." Lyrics from the classic hymn "In the Garden," along with similar songs, poems, and stories, stirred in me a longing to feel, if not see, Divine Presence as I learned about God's loving protection and mercy. Like the psalmists of the Hebrew scriptures, I prayed for help when I needed to feel safe or when I was in trouble. God became my bodyguard.

God the Bodyguard is the God many people rely upon for protection and comfort. Many people I know have matured in human ways but have clung to the Bodyguard as their primary conceptualization of the divine. Popular prayers and poems reinforce this image. In "Footprints in the Sand," Mary Stevenson put these words into the mouth of the divine: "The times when you have seen only one set of footprints in the sand is when I carried you."

The Prayer for Protection, written by spiritual teacher and poet James Dillet Freeman declares, "The presence of God watches over me." One of numerous promises conveyed by biblical prophets is this passage, intended to soothe the exiled Israelites: "As a mother comforts her child, so I will comfort you" (Isaiah 66:13).

Images evoked by these words pointed to the Bodyguard looking out for my safety, a presence benevolent toward me and separate from me. The Bodyguard was a hired hand. Sometimes I wanted the Bodyguard on duty, sometimes not. Sometimes I bargained with the Bodyguard. How many times I cried, "Just get me out of this predicament, and I will go to Mass the next four Sundays, stop secretly smoking cigarettes out my bedroom window, and think only kind thoughts about my parents." As if the Bodyguard cared about any of that!

The Incredible Shrinking GOD

In my early twenties, I was a practicing yogi living in an American ashram. My days were devoted to hatha yoga, holistic health, meaningful service, and meditation. One of the meditation techniques I was taught was to gaze at a photograph of the guru for several minutes, then close my eyes, lift my closed eyes to the midpoint of my forehead—the third eye—and allow the guru's image to appear there, in my mind. Later, when my guru taught, "the guru is within," I would chuckle at the thought of my guru shrinking to fit inside my head. Of course I realized this idea was a figure of speech, at least I'd like to think I did.

Although my religious education up to that time had located the divine elsewhere, I easily accepted this idea as natural, as natural as my human DNA coming from my earthly father and mother. I believed Jesus Christ's teaching that GOD can be found within: "The Father who dwells in me does His works" (John 14:10). Spiritual teachers through the ages have echoed Jesus's message. The writer of the Bible's book of Colossians emphasized the mystery of "Christ in you, the hope of glory" (Colossians 1:27b). Meister Eckhart, a 13th-century Christian mystic, declared, "You need not look for God either here or there. He is no farther away than the door of your heart."

During years of yoga meditation practice, I developed a voracious desire to know the divine within me. In transcendent moments, I did know. I had no words to describe the experience except that I perceived no person, certainly no "He." Rather, I felt at one with everything and everyone. I felt whole.

Later I was introduced to Unity, a spiritual movement emphasizing that GOD is Oneness and that we are one with GOD. When I learned Unity cofounder Charles Fillmore's invocation, I found a new way to understand the internalized divine of my meditations: "I am now in the presence of pure Being; immersed in the Holy Spirit of Life, Love, and Wisdom ..." Oh, I realized, GOD is Divine Life, Divine Love, and Divine Wisdom within me!

It was comforting to believe I could go within. I carried GOD with me all the time. Yet, the idea of an incredible shrinking GOD seemed incomplete. The divine could not be limited by the borders of my body and the boundaries of my comprehension. Furthermore, I wanted a GOD bigger than me.

Divine Omnipresence

By the time I had graduated from Catholicism, invested three years in intensive yoga training, and begun metaphysical studies in Unity, I had absorbed the wonderful truth of the divine as an indwelling presence. Unity Sunday services and classes all began with the call to go within. Answers to my questions could be found within. I knew this. I also knew answers could come from a conversation with a friend, through an advertisement on a billboard, from a dream, or in any number of ways logical and illogical. Divine Life, Love, and Wisdom resided within me, certainly. Also, Divine Life, Love, and Wisdom resided everywhere else.

I had been a resident at the Kripalu ashram for nearly three years when my college sweetheart, Giles, and I reconnected and decided to marry. A trusted adviser recommended I participate in the ashram's four-day inner quest intensive, in order to become conscious and clear about my choice. The intensive incorporated Gestalt and '70s-style personal transformation modalities. Every detail of the intensive was designed to quickly peel off exterior concerns, getting down to raw emotion where limiting core beliefs could be recognized and released. Windows in the rooms we occupied were covered with brown paper, clocks were removed, mealtimes and rest times were deliberately manipulated to confuse bodies and brains that thrive on routine. In this setting, I faced my excuses for getting married. With the support of a facilitator's probing questions, I realized:

> I long for Disney's "happily ever after."
>
> I want to be taken care of.
>
> I fear being alone.
>
> I don't want to be responsible for myself.
>
> I need someone else to love me in ways I do not love myself.
>
> I do not love myself.
>
> I do not trust myself.
>
> I am not enough.
>
> I am terrified of being alone because I am not enough.

Deeper and deeper I went into a dark, empty, isolated state. I went to a reality that seemed devoid of anything, even the divine. I was totally alone. Moreover, no one else could give me all I felt

I lacked. Spiritual freedom as well as human happiness could not be conferred on me by anyone else, not even by the divine. I would have to love myself. I would have to love myself! Doubled over in spiritual pain, I curled up on the floor in the fetal position. I was utterly alone. Despondent. Disappearing. Dying.

A warm hand covered mine, a soft voice saying "Come with me." One of my ashram sisters practically carried me to my bunk, laid me down, sat with me, and stroked my hair. I filled up with love. She became Divine Love for me.

The more I thought about it, the more I began to notice Divine Life, Love, and Wisdom appearing in unexpected moments, in surprising ways. Several years later, bedridden for four weeks with pericarditis, an inflammation of the fluid surrounding the heart, I continued to notice Divine Life, Love, and Wisdom in the faces of the divine appearing at my side, tending to my every need. Every day brought new insights about my life, including my increasing capacity to relax and let Divine Love in. Divine Wisdom was revealing the benefit of extended rest and renewal. I received this temporary condition as a gift of Divine Presence, true to Jesus's proclamation in the Gospel of Thomas that "the kingdom of the heavens is within you and all around you" (3:6b). This kingdom came to me.

One of the most moving moments in film, I believe, occurred toward the end of *Dead Man Walking* when Sister Helen Prejean heard Matthew's pre-execution confession. Matthew revealed that despite self-condemnation and his expectation of eternal damnation, he had prayed for the kids he had murdered. Sister Helen, with full-on eye contact, spoke with spiritual authority to the convict. She said, "You are a son of God, Matthew Poncelet." He broke down. No one had ever told him.

Turns out, the divine can be found in murderers as well as in masters. In pain as well as in pleasure. In failure as much as in success.

Divine Omnipresence means GOD is within us, we are within GOD, and GOD is everywhere. Moreover, GOD is everywhere-ness, not a being who is everywhere but the pervasive essence of all, as suggested by 17th-century Hindu mystic Ramadasa:

> *Wherever you cast your glance,*
> *it is before you.*
> *You in fact see within it.*
> *It is both inside and outside.*
> *Where we feel it is not,*
> *it immediately manifests itself.*
> *Whatever object we take in hand—*
> *it is nearer to us than that.*

With these realizations, GOD as a person ceased to exist for me. I stopped referring to GOD as God. Instead, I began relating to the divine as Divine Life, Love, and Wisdom. "God is Principle," Myrtle Fillmore, cofounder of Unity, wrote in *How to Let God Help You*. "God is not a cold, senseless principle like that of mathematics, but the Principles of Life, Love, and Intelligence."

The *I AM*

I came to realize that Divine Life, Love, and Wisdom are not personal; that is, they do not register in my thinking as GOD coming down to my size, fitting within the confines of my body and brain. Still, Divine Life, Love, and Wisdom seemed to be something other than *me* living in me or flowing from me. I felt disturbed by the possibility that some force could blow through me perhaps without my consent. When I heard people say after praying aloud, "Those were not my words but the words of the Spirit flowing through me," I cringed. I cringed because I sensed a false modesty in their words. I knew they were not disinterested bystanders but active participants in expressing the wisdom of their words. I too have experienced moments when inexplicable wisdom has flowed from me.

When I was a practicing massage therapist, it was not uncommon for me to feel from within my hands the places of greatest pain in my clients' bodies or to get a persistent thought about them that would not quit until I asked their permission to share it. In my pastoral ministry, I frequently feel a consciousness shift before delivering a potent Sunday message or entering a hospital room for a prayerful visit.

But . . . but . . . but . . . Am I unnecessary to these occurrences? Am I under a spell, so to speak, during these moments so that "something" comes over me? Can these phenomena occur without my cooperation?

No! *I am* present. *I am* feeling the truth before I speak it. *I AM.*

Rev. Dr. Paul Hasselbeck, dean of Unity spiritual education and enrichment at Unity Institute, upgraded Charles Fillmore's invocation to reveal the truth in it: "I AM the presence of Pure Beingness; expressing the whole spirit of Life, Love, and

Wisdom." *I AM* is the Divine Name. *I AM* is the Divine Life, Love, and Wisdom.

I settled on the understanding that I AM Divine Life, Love, and Wisdom expressed.

I AM.

The Ineffable

The Most High. The True Light. Divine Mind. Source. The Holy One. Infinite Love. I cannot define it, but I have experienced it. Perhaps you have experienced it too.

Poets and mystics of every culture and faith tradition have attempted to describe the indescribable, the ineffable Divine Nature. Formless yet capable of taking any form; unseen yet appearing in visions; unknowable yet revealing itself to devotees; timeless yet pondered in every era—the confusing yet compelling Divine Nature.

We try and we try to understand the incomprehensible!

In the Bhagavad Gita (Hindu scripture), the mythological warrior Arjuna glimpses the True Nature of Lord Krishna. Arjuna exclaims: "You are the knower, the known, and the state beyond knowing—all the universe is filled by you, O Lord of Infinite Forms."

The Koran (6:103) teaches: "No vision can grasp Him, but His grasp is over all vision; He is above all comprehension, yet is acquainted with all things." ('Abdullah Yūsuf 'Alī, *The Meaning of the Holy Qur'ān*, 10th ed. [Beltsville, MD: Amana Publications, 1999].)

A hymn from the Twa, a central-African tribe, proclaims:

Who can make an image of God?
He has no body.
He is as a word which comes out of your mouth.
That word! It is no more,
It is past, and still it lives!
So is God.

(Molefi Kete Asante and Ama Mazama [Eds.]*Encyclopedia of African Religion*, vol. 2 [Thousand Oaks, CA: Sage, 2009])

In the Bible, Job pondered, "Can you find out the deep things of God? Can you find out the limit of the Almighty? It is higher than heaven—what can you do? Deeper than Sheol—what can you know? Its measure is longer than the earth, and broader than the sea" (Job 11:7–9).

Each of these references points to the indescribable, ineffable Divine Nature. Why do we care about the divine? Why do we quest and question? Why do we hunger to understand Divine Nature? For one reason: Divine Nature is our True Nature. As Jesus Christ is reported to have taught, "You are the light of the world" (Matthew 5:14). "Is it not written in your law, 'I said, you are gods'?" (John 10:34). All that GOD is is our True Nature. We are divine.

Your Divine Identity

Our words and methods of prayer derive from our sense of identity. When we view ourselves as "only human," we pray to God from a consciousness of powerlessness. When we realize our Divine Identity, we pray from the Divine Consciousness.

You Are Not a Sinner

I delivered my second child in a hospital birthing room. I worked long and hard for seventeen hours, eventuating with the primal push and groan of delivery. Giles was first to behold the seven pounds of wrinkles-with-girl-parts. Giles cut the cord, gathered up her crumpled body, and laid her in a warm bath.

I turned my head and watched, mesmerized along with Giles, as our baby's toes uncurled and turned pink—then her legs, her belly, her torso, arms, and fingers one by one pinkening and stretching. Finally, her face filled out, evidence of life flushed her cheeks, and her eyes opened along with her mouth as her healthy lungs brought forth a demanding cry. Giles wrapped her in a soft blanket and placed her in my arms. She turned her dazzling little face up to mine. In that moment, captivated, I spoke the words that I knew were on everyone's mind—the doctor's, her daddy's, the nurse's. I cried out, "God help you, you miserable little sinner!"

All right, all right, I did not say that. Who would say such a thing? Who would think such a thing? All I knew and all I saw was this marvelous bundle of possibility. I saw the purest expression of love in human form. I saw the beauty of absolute perfection.

No religion except Christianity condemns a person before they behave badly!

If you grew up in Christianity, chances are you learned that Christianity contributes to, and may be the origin of, the idea that humanity is fundamentally ungodly. The "sin gene" passes from one generation to the next so that, according to many Christian denominations, every newborn enters this world corrupted by inherent sinfulness. *The Southern Baptist Theological Seminary Abstract of Principles* (1858) teaches that God originally made humanity in God's own image, free from sin. Humans fell from our original holiness and righteousness, however, when we disobeyed God under the influence of Satan. "His posterity inherit a nature corrupt and wholly opposed to God and His law, are under condemnation, and as soon as they are capable of moral action, become actual transgressors" (VI). By this doctrine, a person is damned from birth.

Roman Catholicism concurs. Catholicism teaches that everyone is born with a fallen human nature and tainted by original sin, making every individual unworthy of being a child of God. A baby is baptized as soon as possible after birth so that, through the act of baptism, the taint of sin can be erased.

Interestingly, Judaism rejects the notion of original sin, believing that the image of God in which humans have been created means humans can think, reason, and choose. Having a dual nature, and free will, humans sometimes choose "good" and sometimes choose "evil."

Islam points to the sin of Adam and Eve, their repentance and forgiveness, as an example of what not to do. Muslims learn that they will be tempted by the devil, but they will be less likely to sin when they are faithful to the Koran.

Eastern religions do not subscribe to a doctrine of sin. Comparative religions expert Ernest Valea teaches that in Hinduism, ignorance gives rise to poor conduct, the remedy of which is guidance rather than damnation. Everyone is born with the Divine Nature and the capacity to live into that Nature.

That we in the Western world have inherited the consequences of Adam and Eve's sin seems a little unfair. It reminds me of the times one of my six siblings misbehaved, when we were children, and all of us got sent to our rooms without supper. Belief in the sin gene permeates the Western world. We have produced a culture of shame. Exasperated parents—the same parents who beheld the perfection at their children's births—point fingers at their children: *Bad boy! Bad girl! You should be ashamed of yourself! Who do you think you are?*

As children, we internalized shame. We still carry guilt and shame, even if "only" within our subconscious, retained from times in the past when we heard those words or adopted them by misinterpreting someone's message. How often each of us thinks, *I'll never be good enough. I can't seem to do anything right. I'm a loser.*

Even at fifty years of age and older, we might still try to prove to our parents that we are worthy, because we ourselves do not believe we *are* worthy. We attempt in every way to measure up to someone else's expectations. Even when we achieve a goal or accomplish some good, we ask, *Who am I to be successful?* Or, ironically, we hear the voices of our families telling us, as they've told us before, *You're getting too big for your britches; come down off your high horse.*

We do not intend to demean ourselves with guilt and shame. We do not consciously agree with these ideas. They are imbedded falsehoods that we have presumed to be true. They do not originate with us, although they tap into our deepest human insecurity, which is for many of us fed by religious doctrine. We do not intend to diminish our children's sense of identity, either. In fact, never in my life have I met anyone who believes, really, that their children could have inherited the sin gene.

You Are Divine

We do not believe in the sin gene because we know, inherently, that we are divine.

An eagle egg, if it could be self-aware, might behold a mature eagle spiraling upward on a current of warm air and think to itself: *I'll never fly like that. Eggs cannot fly.* That's right, they never will. But eggs can hatch into eagles.

The yolk of an eagle egg contains the genetic code for *eagle*. Eagle is its true identity. The shell of an eagle egg hardens into a protective crust around the chick-in-progress. The chick must at some point emerge from the shell, casting it off, in order to grow and finally to fly.

Spiritually speaking, the shell can be equated with a person's external sense of self covering his true self. Through spiritual practices such as prayer and meditation, an individual breaks open the corporeal, only-human identity as she realizes her eternal spiritual identity, her true self. In the same way we mature humanly by realizing, increasingly, our human capacities, we mature spiritually by expressing, increasingly, our Divine Nature. Charles Fillmore taught

> It is your mission to express all that you can imagine
> God to be. Let this be your standard of achievement;
> never lower it, nor allow yourself to be belittled by the
> cry of sacrilege. You can attain to everything you can
> imagine. If you can imagine that it is possible to God, it
> is also possible to you.

We have the hearts of Divine Love, the minds of Divine Wisdom, the lives of Divine Life. Since the divine is not a person but a principle and we are made in a divine image, the Love Principle, the Wisdom Principle, and the Life Principle are our nature. We identify ourselves as these principles. We claim Divine Identity.

Identification with our roles, relationships, and conditions results in false identities precisely because roles, relationships, and conditions are temporary and changeable. For example, my current role as parent to my two children is significantly different in their adulthood from what it was in their childhood. They no longer need me to keep food on the table, but they ask my advice when they're buying their own kitchen tables. I have changed careers three times. I had a trim, petite body when I married Giles more than thirty years ago and, well, let's just say there is more of me to love nowadays. But my true identity is changeless, permanent—made in a divine image and likeness—and not conditional to the between-the-lines human inference *only when you behave perfectly!*

> We have the hearts of Divine Love, the minds of Divine Wisdom, the lives of Divine Life. The Love Principle, the Wisdom Principle, and the Life Principle are our nature. We identify ourselves as these principles. We claim Divine Identity.

You are made in the divine image. This is an irrevocable truth. Your True Nature is divine. You are destined to grow up to this realization, to identify yourself as divine.

I can illustrate this idea with a story about something real and tangible. In the fifties, a community of Buddhist monks learned that a road would be built precisely at the site of a shrine housing a gigantic clay statue of the Buddha. The crane brought in to relocate the statue was not up to the task and cracked the statue in several places. The monks called for a larger crane, but it would not arrive until the following day. Rain was expected overnight. The monks covered the statue as best they could before retiring for the night.

During the night one of the monks took his lantern outside to check on the site. When the light fell upon the statue, the monk noticed a glow between some of the cracks. He returned indoors for a hammer and a chisel with which to carve away a little of the clay. Astonished at what was revealed, the monk ran back to the sleeping quarters and awakened the entire community. Everyone chipped away at the statue, revealing beneath the clay exterior a solid-gold Buddha statue. The monks surmised that the gold statue had been covered with clay centuries earlier to protect it from being confiscated during war.

Our external identities are like the clay surrounding that golden Buddha. Charles Fillmore taught, "We are all, in our personality, wearing the mask that conceals the real, the spiritual, *I AM*." (Charles Fillmore, *Jesus Christ Heals* [Forgotten Books, 2008], 102.) Unconsciously a person crafts an external identity, a personality that fits in with other personalities. He molds thoughts, words, and actions to gain approval from a disapproving family. She pretends to be as tough as she thinks she needs to be to survive in a dangerous world. He nods in agreement when one friend gossips about another, while his heart is screaming no. She unknowingly hides her golden true self under the clay cover of acceptability.

All the while, Divine Identity is intact, complete, and immutable. All that you will ever need of it is within you already, and you do not need to go in search of it as though you had gotten separated from it. You are not divine potential but the fullness of Divine Nature.

In any moment you can realize and live from your Divine Identity. You do not have to acquire your Divine Identity; you have only to mature in your understanding of this true identity and claim it.

Claim Your Divine Identity

You recall the Bible stories about the prophets Elijah and Elisha? I call my daughter the prophet Alicia. One evening a couple of years ago, Alicia called me from her apartment in Chicago. She had just turned off the television after watching the show *Primetime*. On the program, a man showed video clips of troubling occurrences, asking the audience to ponder, "What would you do?" in those situations. Alicia was in tears as she recounted one of the clips depicting a homeless elderly man being beaten by a group of young men. The reason she was so upset? Because, she cried, "I don't know how I would answer that question! I would like to think I would do the right thing, but I am afraid I would run the other way instead."

The following afternoon, Alicia called again, which was unusual since we usually stuck with weekly chats. "You won't believe what happened today!" she said. As she did every weekday morning, Alicia had taken the train to the bus stop, where she would transfer and continue on to her job as a teacher. Alicia waited along with others at the stop, which was located in front of a middle school. While waiting, Alicia overheard a group of students talking among themselves. She started to feel uncomfortable as their voices rose and their conversation turned violent. Suddenly, the biggest of the boys turned and began pummeling the smallest boy. Alicia responded instinctively. She ran over to the boys and attempted to pull them away from each other. She shouted, "Stop!" over and over as she continued to tug at the arms of the big teenager. Then, as suddenly as it began, the skirmish came to a halt. The big kid turned his attention to Alicia, an incredulous look in his eyes. Alicia stared him down, undaunted by his bravado. The boy dropped his eyes, turned, and walked away. Recounting the story to me over the telephone, Alicia marveled, "Mom, I did it! I answered the question!"

Alicia may have felt astonished by her instinctive response in this situation, but I was not surprised, for I had witnessed her true self in action throughout her life. The prophet Alicia has always been my teacher. She has a built-in sensitivity toward others that confirms her Divine Identity. She is a magnificent expression of Divine Life, Love, and Wisdom.

Seeing so clearly Alicia's Divine Identity, I find it hard to believe that she does not see it. Like most people, Alicia recognizes her shortcomings more readily than she does her strengths, her mistakes more easily than her accomplishments. She does not believe that her Divine Identity is intact and independent of her actions. She thinks she has to qualify for Divine Nature. I tell her, "Just as you are, you are magnificent! Just as you are, you are divine!"

Just as *you* are, you are magnificent! Just as *you* are, you are divine!

We have misunderstood the great truth about Divine Identity. We have called it "potential" as if we have to work toward the goal of divinity. We have believed it to be conditional, as if each of us could gain or lose individual Divine Identity depending upon individual actions. We have thought we have to journey to find our Divine Identity, as if it had gotten lost or separated from us. We do not have to claim our Divine Identity in order to have Divine Identity. But what good is a Divine Identity if a person does not claim it?

You claim your Divine Identity moment by moment, choice by choice. What you know yourself to be in any moment determines your approach to prayer.

What good is a talent for music if a person never plays an instrument? The talent is intact, but it must be claimed if it would be expressed and enjoyed. Deciding not to play music does not make someone evil, nor is the person punished for that choice. The music remains in that person, latent until she chooses to express it.

When will you claim your Divine Identity? When you have the choice of how to respond to someone's hurtful remark, will you throw back angry words, or will you express Divine Life, Love, and Wisdom? When feeling tempted to judge your appearance harshly in the mirror, will you instead gaze through to the Divine Life, Love, and Wisdom reflected there?

You claim your Divine Identity moment by moment, choice by choice. What you know yourself to be in any moment determines your approach to prayer.

Talk to Yourself

- What did you believe about God when you were a child? How have your childhood beliefs about God influenced your adulthood?

- Write or speak of a time you experienced the divine in another person, and then in yourself.

- Remember a mystical moment when something of Divine Nature was revealed to you. How did your understanding of the divine change from the experience?

- When you address God, regardless of the name and nature you ascribe to God at the time (Gracious Father, Sweet Spirit, Dear God, Infinite Love, etc.), what are you supposing about Divinity, or Divine Nature? About yourself?

- How might you describe your Divine Identity without personifying the divine?

Chapter 2

Learn Affirmative Prayer

Prayer is not a means of arousing God to action but the process of waking up from our drowsiness so we can see ourselves, not in a mirror darkly but face-to-face.

—*Eric Butterworth, renowned Unity leader*

We pray, asserting our Divine Identity so we may express our Divine Identity. We pray so that we embody Divine Nature.

During one of the longest six-month stretches of my life, I had reason to assert my Divine Identity as never before. My approach to and practice of prayer changed abruptly, dramatically. First, in October 2002 my husband was laid off from the best-paying position he had ever held—the technology field was suffering from stock plunges and company bankruptcies. Our mortgage depended upon his salary. We sold our home and down-sized immediately. Within weeks of our move, the Unity church

I was serving as the associate pastor fired me for insubordination when I would not sign a waiver of liability insurance for spiritual counseling I conducted within the scope of my pastoral responsibilities. And since the ministerial training program I had begun several months earlier required me to be an associate pastor within a spiritual community, my ministerial training was also suspended.

My anxiety about home and career became overshadowed by my most pressing concern: my son was in Iraq. Adrian, a US marine, had deployed with other first-in troops during the 2002 year-end holidays. On March 20, 2003, the dreaded news came that US troops had mobilized to occupy Iraq. Adrian provided logistics support to a reconnaissance unit. He was a moving target in a Humvee while his comrades convoyed in armored tanks. Thankfully, I did not know this at the time, nor did I realize Adrian and his unit were being ambushed nightly along the treacherous route to Baghdad. I did, however, watch the news from morning till night in search of word about his unit from an embedded reporter.

At the convergence of these events, I was given the gift of a spiritual counseling session from a highly regarded professional. Eager for some support, I walked in, sat down, and started spewing all my woes. Crying, worrying, wanting someone to say, *Poor baby*.

Instead I was slapped across the face—spiritually speaking—when the counselor remarked, "So, you don't really believe there is only One Presence and One Power. You don't really believe that you are divine and therefore able to walk through the uncertainties of this time in confidence. You don't really believe that you and your son are Divine Love, inseparable whether he is in Iraq or off the planet."

Instead of running away as I felt inclined to do, I remained rooted to my seat. Instead of receiving the counselor's words as an attack, I swiftly shifted into alignment with the truth he was illuminating. I sat up straight, wiped the tears away from my cheeks, and whispered, "Thank you." I left that session prepared to seek my next rightful place of service and to practice Oneness in meditation twice each day in front of a photograph of my son.

I received a gift from spiritual counseling in the form of a strong reminder to return to the principles I had been practicing for several years. These principles had been easy to uphold during times of stability and easy to abandon when I felt overwhelmed by shifting conditions. Now, with renewed fervor, I practiced to prove the power of these spiritual principles to transform, sustain, and enliven me.

Instead of worrying about how my husband and I would pay our bills, I began affirming in prayer the amazing abundance of good in my life. Then I expressed appreciation every time I had the funds to pay the bills due. Instead of feeling helpless to ensure my son's safety while he served in Iraq, through prayer I recognized the powerful magnet of Divine Love that I AM, the harmony of Divine Love that brings all things—and all beings—together for good, the unity of Divine Love that makes us one. Instead of asking a superhuman God to change the conditions of my life at that time, I affirmed my Divine Identity, the powers and capacities I am here to bring into visibility. Those months turned out to be among the most spiritually focused high times of my life—when

I embodied my Divine Identity intentionally and saved myself the anguish typical for people in such circumstances.

Why We Pray

Once each year in the spiritual community where I am minister, the trained prayer chaplains choose whether to continue in their roles for another year, and if they decide in the affirmative, they repeat the extensive training along with newcomers to the team. One year one prayer chaplain opted to repeat the training before determining whether she would serve another year. The reason for her hesitancy became clear during a practice prayer session when the chaplain posed this question: "If GOD is not a person, and if my nature is divine, why would I pray?"

Good question!

We knew why and how we prayed when we thought of GOD as a superhuman. When we were in pain, we prayed in hopes God would grant us relief. When we worried about a loved one, we prayed, asking God to save, to heal, or to fix our loved one. When we felt wronged by another person's actions, we wanted God to give that person what he deserved. When we lost hope, we prayed, looking for God to grant us a miracle. As Charles Fillmore said, "We have been so persistently taught that prayer consists in asking God for some human need that we have lost sight of our spiritual identity and have become a race of praying beggars."

We believed in a capricious God sometimes saying yes and other times no. We believed in an arbitrary God permitting wrongdoers to prosper and innocents to suffer. We believed in a co-dependent God watching with sadness as we forced our way through life, waiting for the day when we would ask his help. We believed in a sadistic God getting his kicks from counting our sins.

When we thought of GOD as a superhuman, we imagined a human with a personality and supernatural powers—a comic-book superhero! We thought the purpose of prayer was to get God's attention and convince him to do us a favor. Prayer seemed useful when we thought God would be reluctant to provide our every need or unwilling to give us all we wanted; we believed we had to prove our worthiness to God. Now we know better about GOD.

GOD is not a person. We personally, individually, express GOD as we realize and embody Divine Life, Love, Intelligence, and all the Divine Capacities.

GOD is not a person. We personally, individually, express GOD as we realize and embody Divine Life, Love, Intelligence, and all the Divine Capacities. GOD is the One Power in all and through all, Life Itself, Love Itself, the indescribable yet recognizable Divine Force. The divine *is* the invisible Good we can choose to make visible. This understanding prompts a new *why* and a new *how* to pray.

Why We Stop Praying

As spiritual understanding evolves, we must discover a new reason to pray and learn a new way to pray. If not, we may become discouraged, until we stop praying altogether. We stop praying when we feel confused about the purpose of prayer, unworthy to claim our Divine Identity, or disillusioned when we do not see the benefit of prayer.

My children grew up in Unity. In our family, we practiced the principles of Unity, including the understanding there is only One Presence, One Power, and One Divine Nature that we are. To my astonishment, several years after my son, Adrian, left home, he told me, "I have no desire to step foot in church ever again." I was curious about his reasoning for such a strong statement. Adrian enlightened me by saying "All everybody at church ever wanted was to fix me, but nothing is wrong with me, and I do not need to be fixed." Well, on the one hand, I wanted to reach my arms up to the sky and shout, "That's right! Nothing is wrong with you. You are divine!" On the other hand, I felt gut-punched because all along I had thought we were successfully teaching Adrian about his Divine Identity.

As I thought more about Adrian's experience, I recognized that while we had spoken about Divine Nature and our Divine Identity when Adrian was growing up, we had not known how to pray claiming our Divine Identity. Therefore, we could not have taught Adrian how to identify with his Divine Nature. We had not known to say to Adrian, prayer is not about other people wanting you to be better (although I daresay it was on my mind throughout Adrian's teen years). Prayer is about you enjoying a better life empowered by your Divine Capacities. Claiming your Divine Identity during tough times leads to greater life, greater love, and greater good, all of which are natural for you to desire because they are your True Nature.

What Adrian had internalized was the erroneous message that prayer is about repairing a flawed human nature rather than about claiming a Divine Nature. No wonder Adrian resisted! Who wouldn't resist a notion totally contrary to the reality of our Divine Identity!

Confusion about the purpose of prayer can be discouraging, but unworthiness in prayer makes it impossible to claim our rightful Divine Identity. Joanie (not her real name) attended my six-week course on affirmative prayer. She was new to my spiritual community and clearly struggling through teachings that were unfamiliar to her. Joanie completed the course and then left the community, returning to a traditional church. She told me she felt uncomfortable claiming a Divine Identity. She felt great comfort and relief turning her worries over to God and trusting that God would make everything all right. Joanie felt unworthy. She would never compare her nature with God's. She was not GOD. She was only human.

Many of us experience disillusionment in prayer because we do not realize the benefit of prayer. It may appear our prayers are not answered when people die anyway, we continue to feel angry in our relationships, or we do not get instant relief from financial stress. However, the issue has never been whether prayer is answered—how we live is the issue and the answer! We are the answer to our prayers as we realize prayer is not a plea for a particular outcome but a calling upon ourselves to realize what we are to *be* in a circumstance. For example, when praying about a loved one's illness, you may be inspired to be Divine Life expressing wholeness and beholding the wholeness of your loved one. When praying about your relationship, you can be Divine Love releasing separateness-consciousness and cultivating harmonious feelings. When praying about your financial circumstances, you might realize you are Divine Abundance blessing every dollar coming in and going out.

For many of us whose understanding of the divine has evolved, we have not yet learned to pray in a way that is congruent with our elevated understanding. Many New Thought teachers' prayers resemble traditional prayer. Students are rightfully confused when they are told we pray from a Divine Consciousness and then hear the salutation "Dear God." My desire in the following pages is to offer a singular purpose for prayer and a way of achieving this purpose.

One Purpose in Prayer

We may think we pray for relief from pain and painful feelings, to gain reassurance during times of doubt and worry, or to plead for something or someone to be changed. When we are ready to evolve beyond that fallacy, we have to reframe our purpose for prayer. In the past we would have pleaded with God to heal our pain, but now our prayer intention is to embody our Divine Capacity for wholeness. We know that Divine Nature is wholeness and Divine Nature is ours. Therefore we are made from Divine Wholeness. We have the Divine Capacity to experience wholeness in the midst of all circumstances, including painful ones. We discover through prayer that pain is a passing condition, whereas wholeness is independent of fleeting conditions. Pain recedes in the face of spiritual realization. Wholeness flows continuously.

A few years ago, I required a new purpose for prayer. Having raised my children, prayed my way through my son's four years in the military, lived beyond my first half century, achieved Unity ordination, passed my five-year anniversary as a minister of Unity in San Antonio, and reached year thirty in my marriage, I had many reasons to feel fulfilled. Every dimension of my life pulsed with purpose. The drama meter rarely signaled. Life hummed.

I got restless. I began to sense that feeling fulfilled was overrated, or at least it was temporary and fading fast. *What next? What else?* became a new drumbeat within, growing bolder and more emphatic every day. Thinking the drama meter was signaling, I tried ignoring those feelings of restlessness. Instead, I sat through my daily prayer practice experiencing less and less satisfaction. I could not pray to God, because by then I was sure GOD was not a superhuman listening to my complaints. I could not comprehend GOD as a nonperson, but I certainly had no way to pray if not to a superhuman. I went through the motions, pressing on in ways I had learned to do during times of spiritual drought. All the while I, an ordained minister, was feeling disillusioned about the most fundamental spiritual practice. I recited empty affirmations in the hopes they would stimulate some inspiration. Meanwhile, I fantasized about leaving my husband, running away from my church, reneging on my responsibilities, and ditching my friends.

Unhappy in every way, I reached out for support. I found a wonderful therapist, who assisted me in making sense of my emotions. I received powerful prayer support and gained insight from my spiritual counselor, who listened as I talked through the spiritual implications of my emotional depression.

Over time, I noticed that dissatisfaction with my work and home life were symptoms rather than primary concerns. Nothing was wrong with my church or my husband. I started to see there was one common denominator in all my unhappy circumstances: me!

Darn it, don't you hate that? My understanding of Divine Nature had been evolving, but I had been wavering in accepting Divine Nature as *my* nature. I suffered from incongruence, teaching about Divine Identity but failing to claim Divine Identity consistently in prayer or in daily living. Furthermore, I struggled for authenticity as a spiritual leader, uncomfortable speaking words of spiritual authority without feeling them alive within me. I strove tirelessly to rise above self-doubt and disillusionment when providing spiritual direction to others. I could see in others their Divine Identity and even offer them spiritual strategies for thinking and acting accordingly, but I was in the midst of a profound period of questioning that appeared to me endless and tedious.

Pragmatist that I am, I probed and journaled and conversed and meditated my way up and out of suffering. I committed myself to praying anew, to being authentic in prayer. I agreed to study prayer more intently to gain spiritual understanding and new purpose. I thought if I am one with GOD, and GOD is Love, then I AM Love! I contemplated the meaning of Divine Love. I claimed Divine Love as my True Nature. I began realizing how Divine Love moves in me, how Divine Love behaves in the world. My awareness of the Divine Love that I AM grew; it was like a vein receiving a blood transfusion. As new blood revitalizes the body, Divine Love revitalized me. Amazingly, my mood

We pray for one reason and one reason only. All reasons for prayer can be distilled down to one: We pray to claim and assert our Divine Identity so that we can live more fully from it. We pray so that we may embody Divine Nature.

began to lift. I became interested once again in my Divine Identity and the Divine Identity of others. I realized this is the purpose of prayer: to assert my Divine Identity.

In the same way, I contemplated Divine Life, Divine Wisdom, Divine Power, Divine Order, and all the attributes of the divine. Claiming Divine Capacities became my daily prayer practice, far more empowering than "mea culpa" and "Lord, I am not worthy."

I came to realize we pray for one reason and one reason only. All reasons for prayer can be distilled down to one: We pray to claim and assert our Divine Identity so that we can live more fully from it. We pray so that we may embody Divine Nature. This type of prayer is called affirmative prayer. Although I had been teaching about prayer for years, my realizations about affirmative prayer led to renewed passion that ignited desire for prayer practice in the minds and hearts of my students.

Affirmative Prayer Is Not Your Traditional Prayer

Affirmative prayer is not your traditional prayer. Traditional prayer methods in Christian denominations and various other world religions share commonalities that are not found in affirmative prayer. Traditional prayer does the following:

- approaches the divine as a personality, a kind of human with superhuman powers;
- beseeches, attempts to convince a divine personality to supply a need or desire; and
- presumes a divine personality that is hesitant, capricious, withholding, and that must be persuaded; and

- bargains with a divine personality, promising good behavior in exchange for favors.

Affirmative prayer, on the other hand, does not involve begging a distant God to change ourselves, other people, or our circumstances. Affirmative prayer does the following:

- cultivates our awareness of Oneness, the One Power and Presence, and Divine Mind; we pray from a consciousness of GOD;
- identifies Divine Nature as our True Nature; we claim our Divine Identity; and
- reveals the highest truth we can comprehend in this moment; we realize the truth.

Pray from a Consciousness of GOD

> To pray truly one must enter into God consciousness, must rise in mind to the plane of Spirit. If the prayers we offer are full of requests for things, we are in a consciousness of materiality, and we are addressing our prayers to a false god that has no power to answer them.
> —*Frances W. Foulks, Unity teacher,* Effectual Prayer *(1945)*

To pray from a consciousness of GOD is to acknowledge Divine Nature so we may assume that nature—identify ourselves as divine. The simplest way do this is to contemplate what we already know about Divine Nature. We know a lot about Divine Nature, not necessarily in religious terms but through experiences. Following are some examples:

We know Divine Nature is as invisible yet as evident as the air we breathe. At any time the free flow of air is curtailed, we notice its absence. More real than material air, however, is All That Is, or Divine Nature. Divine Nature is an inexhaustible, ever-flowing current. Real, yet unseen; invisible, yet essential.

We know Divine Nature as omnipresence, or everywhereness. Unity's late poet laureate James Dillet Freeman coined the phrase "Wherever I am, GOD is."

We know Divine Nature as omniscience. It's not as though GOD is a person holding the key to all knowledge. Knowledge is divine. The capacity to know is divine.

We know Divine Nature as omnipotence. GOD is not an all-powerful superhuman; that is why the adage "God is in charge" is erroneous. Instead of feeling fearful of a God who controls everything from weather to war, we recognize GOD is power. Divine Power is spiritual authority. It is spiritual confidence and courageous action. It is mastery over thoughts, also known as spiritual transformation.

Charles Fillmore of Unity identified twelve particular Divine Capacities intrinsic to humanity that, when understood, developed, and practiced, raise human beings above an "only human" existence. The Twelve Powers are Divine Attributes that epitomize this Christian scripture: "The one who is in you is greater than the one who is in the world" (1 John 4:4). Although all of the powers may be expressed "in the world," that is, in literal ways, the Twelve Powers are developed in spiritual practice to be expressed spiritually—in thought or consciousness. Their expression in consciousness leads to transformed living "in the world."

The powers are

Love: power of attraction, harmony, and unity

Strength: power of steadfastness, stability, and endurance

Faith: power of perception, expectation, and assurance

Wisdom/Judgment: power of discernment, discrimination, and evaluation

Power: power of self-mastery, transformation, and confidence

Elimination/Release/Denial: power of release, cleansing, and casting off

Imagination: power of conception, creation, and vision

Understanding: power of recognition, realization, and insight

Will: power of determination, commitment, and willingness

Order: power of adjustment, organization, and balance

Zeal: power of enthusiasm, intensity, and inspiration

Life: power of animation, vitality, and wholeness

In addition to these Divine Powers, we know Divine Nature as peace, joy, abundance, and goodness. Whatever we know GOD to be, we can be.

When we enter a time of prayer with a particular spiritual intention or heart's desire, how do we perceive Divine Nature in regard to this subject, this situation? For instance, when my intention is to express my talents and skills in a fulfilling new job, I consider that Divine Nature is abundance, which means there are infinite ways this intention can be fulfilled. I think about Divine Love as the harmonizing and unifying power and Divine Wisdom as the discerning power, through both of which I am drawn to possibilities in harmony with my highest intention. I recall the numerous times in my life when my intentions were fulfilled beyond my imagination, because I realized Divine Nature is intelligence, omniscience, and unity. In my example of a new job, I recognize that my true desire is not for a job but for a fullness of life that includes being in service, thriving in all ways, and feeling fulfilled. I recognize Divine Nature is Joy, the very Joy that I AM.

Claim Divine Identity in Prayer

Prayer is the most effective method of renewal and transformation, because in prayer [we] associate with God and not with the problem.

—*Myrtle Fillmore, cofounder of Unity; in*
How to Let God Help You *(1956)*

I liken the practice of prayer to tweaking an automobile's radio during a long-distance road trip. Every time we drive out of range, we hear the static signaling it is time to adjust the dial. When feeling attuned to our Divine Identity, we pray so we might remain attuned. We pray with the intention of holding our attention on our spiritual capacities.

We drive out of range easily, don't we? One moment we are saying "All is well." The next moment we are complaining about another driver on the road. One moment we recognize "I am Divine Wholeness." The next moment we sneeze and say, "I must be catching a cold."

Well, you may be thinking, it would be great to feel attuned all the time. But let's get real. Much of the time we forget our Divine Identity in the moment of a human experience. We become mesmerized by material facts, feeling overcome by their seeming power. Unconsciously, in that moment, we are identifying with a circumstance rather than with the divine. We forget that the Divine Power within us is greater than the power in the world.

I have forgotten my Divine Identity during challenging times. I describe throughout these pages various times during which I seemed not to know I possessed a Divine Identity. Each time, I felt I was discovering my Divine Identity for the first time. I believe that spiritual practice eventually leads to a state of continual remembrance of Divine Identity. The great masters, such as Jesus and the Buddha, demonstrated this possibility. Sometimes I forget my Divine Identity, but each time that I come back around to my True Nature, I am spiritually stronger. Spiritual progress may appear as two steps forward, one step back, but it is actually a spiraling upward. The Divine we are is a perpetual movement forward, upward, and onward.

When we forget our Divine Identity, prayer is truly a wonderful tool for recalling our Divine Identity.

All my life I have been directionally challenged. No matter how many years I live in any town, I never master the roads. When I moved to San Antonio, someone handed me a laminated map of major roadways showing the inner and outer loops of the city. I had gotten lost on roads running north and south, east and west. Now I would have to contend with loops! To my relief, I discovered turnarounds on the highways in San Antonio. When I mistakenly drove past my destination, I could exit the highway and turn back around. The turnaround became my friend. I would see the familiar road sign ahead and breathe easier knowing I could choose another direction if needed. Prayer functions like a Texas turnaround: to turn around is the purpose of claiming our Divine Identity. For example, when we regret the words that just came out of our mouth, we can "take two." We can choose again the words we speak. We can call forth from within us our Divine Identity.

When I moved to an American yoga ashram in my early twenties, I began to discover my Divine Identity. Through spiritual practices, including yoga and meditation, I gained inner strength that I expressed as confidence in teaching as well as serenity in the midst of challenges. Effortlessly each day I arose at 4:30 a.m. for spiritual practices, an eager student with a perpetual smile on my face. I practiced silence for days on

When we forget our Divine Identity, prayer is truly a wonderful tool for recalling our Divine Identity.

end, wearing a sign so no one would attempt to talk with me. I felt *spiritual*, floating around the campus in my white sari.

Then, one morning after months and months, I could not get up from my bedroll. I started cleansing, the ashram code word for getting sick. I began craving the peanut butter locked in the communal kitchen walk-in refrigerator, imagining breaking in during the night. I found fault with my roommates and slipped out early from evening satsangs (gatherings for chanting, meditation, and yoga instruction). I was experiencing what in Unity is known as chemicalization. Chemicalization is a confused state of consciousness occurring when embedded beliefs appear threatened by the introduction of new spiritual ideas. I did not enjoy chemicalization. I wanted my spiritual high. I wanted a return to feeling spiritual.

During my first hardcore chemicalization at the ashram, a helpful sister advised me to repeat the mantra "Om namo Bhagavate Vasudevaya" (Srimad Bhagavatam, 1.1.1). Prostrated in front of my personal altar, I chanted these words, interpreted as "I bow to the divine within the Divine Human." Sobbing one moment and reeling with ecstasy the next, I chanted for many hours until I experienced a familiar rhythm of deep peace and confidence that I recognized as my Divine Identity. I arose from my retreat time in spiritual authenticity, feeling reattuned, having turned back around to claim my Divine Identity.

Realize the Higher Truth in Prayer

True prayer brings about an exalted radiation of energy, and when it is accompanied by faith, judgment, and love, the word of Truth bursts forth in a stream of light that, when held in mind, illumines, uplifts, and glorifies.

—*Charles Fillmore,* Prosperity *(1995)*

When a gigantic juicy project, such as writing a book, gets my attention, and I say yes to it, my exhilaration can plummet into terror in no time at all. As I consider all my other magnificent reasons for getting out of bed each morning, I feel my overwhelmed teenaged self having a tantrum. I feel as I did when my mother sat me down when I arrived home from school ready to enroll in another wonderful program—I was already leader of my Girl Scout troop, bassoon player in the high school orchestra, drum major in the boys' high school band, babysitter, poet, summer camp counselor ... You get the picture. Mom mustered up her own mixture of compassion and firmness, saying, "Linda, you know you cannot take on another thing." I banged my fists on the table, indignation rising, shouting out over my tears, "But I want to do it all!" Then, I did not know about my Divine Identity. I did not know I could claim my innate Divine Capacity of wisdom with which I could then decide among many choices.

Today when I feel overwhelmed I pray so that Divine Wisdom rules in my consciousness. Divine Wisdom is my power to discern the best course of action, to discriminate among possibilities, and to choose intelligently. When I feel in my gut an *ah-ha* or *uh-oh*, I can trust my Divine Wisdom and proceed, confidently.

When I sense my son and daughter in emotional pain, the kind of pain that never could be relieved with a bandage and a kiss, I pray so that my mommy brain will not automatically conjure horrible possibilities. I pray so that I remember the truth of their Divine Identity, calling to mind the times I saw them rise higher than their circumstances.

When I receive news of a beloved friend or relative being hospitalized, I pray so that I remain faithful in my thoughts about that person. I pray so that, instead of worrying about outcomes or imagining pain and fear, I hold to and speak of her amazing Divine Life, the Light of the World she is, the capacity of Divine Love that heals all. By my highest thoughts, and in the truth of Oneness, I claim strength to thrive for her.

When I feel uninspired in ministry, I pray so that I remember my calling is not an "only human" intellectual choice but a divine movement, an ever-flowing river rich in Divine Life, Love, and Wisdom. I pray in agreement with my Divine Identity in ministry. I realize the truth of One Presence, One Power flowing from me.

When I feel reluctant to take on an unpleasant but necessary assignment, such as truthfully speaking to another person words I fear he will not want to hear, I pray (claim and assert) that I embody Divine Love and Divine Wisdom. I pray (claim and assert) that I am a living expression of these divine qualities, setting aside my only-human, personal judgments and preferences in that situation.

When I feel alone or afraid, I pray (claim and assert), remembering All That Is, *I AM*. When I feel jealous or lacking, I pray (claim and assert), remembering, *all I could ever want is already mine*. When I feel unhealthy in my body temple, I affirm, *I AM powerful, pulsing Divine Life*. When I feel chaotic, I affirm, *I exist in Divine Order, and I am here to express Divine Order*. When I feel sluggish, I affirm, *I AM limitless Divine Vitality*.

It seems to me that the more we pray for the purpose of remaining attuned to our Divine Identity, the more likely we are to pray when we have forgotten our Divine Identity. Also, the more we pray for the purpose of remaining attuned to our Divine Identity, the less likely we are to forget our Divine Identity. More important, our attunement supports others around us, and all of life. Charles Fillmore taught

> One who has mastered even the primary technique of prayer has made contact with the spiritual ethers that connect all minds, high and low, and by means of which great reforms for the good of man can be projected into the world's thought ether (*Teach Us to Pray*, 16).

Carlo Rossi, fictional mascot for a brand of wine of the same name, remarked in a television commercial, "I like talking about my wine, but I'd rather be drinking it." I could write and you could read all day about affirmative prayer, but we would rather be praying. Let's get started.

Talk to Yourself

- To what degree does praying in a traditional fashion support or detract from your growing awareness of your Divine Identity?

- If you stop saying, in effect, "Dear God, help me to weather this storm" or "Dear God, I ask you to heal my cousin," how might you gain reassurance during prayer?

- What do you know about Divine Nature (the nature of GOD)?

- What do you know about your True Nature? Are you flesh and bones that will one day deteriorate, die, and crumble into dust? Are you a spontaneous creative project, such as a sand castle, that is artistically crafted and then disappears with a single wave crashed up on the shore? Are you a pointless set of circumstances, random and inconsequential? Or are you divine?

Chapter 3

Reform Your Language

Words of Truth are the language of prayer, and if we desire
results in prayer, we must learn to speak its language.

—*Emmet Fox,* The Ten Commandments:
The Master Key to Life *(1953)*

**Your prayers are powerful when conscious, clear, and aligned
with your understanding of the Divine Nature. Reform your
prayer language.**

Words spoken in prayer, whether silent or aloud, have
powerful potential. Words aligned with our spiritual
understanding create congruence in prayer that is
positively transformational. "Prayer is the most highly acceler-
ated mind action known," Charles Fillmore wrote. (*The Revealing
Word* [Unity Books: Unity Village MO, 1959], 138). Of course,

rote prayer, or recitation of familiar prayers, is powerful only to the degree you resonate with the words. For all who have stopped praying or are missing the depth of spiritual fulfillment you once experienced in prayer, it's time to update your words in prayer.

The Power of the Word as Spiritual Principle

"The Word became flesh." This reference to Jesus Christ, from the Gospel of John, is believed by many Christians to equate Jesus with GOD (the Word), come into human form. According to New Thought teachings, Christ was not Jesus's last name but the principle of the Word made flesh, or logos. The Christ is, therefore, the Divine Idea. "It is the real originating center through which man draws all his intelligence, life, love, substance," Fillmore wrote (*Atom-Smashing Power of Mind* [Unity Books: Unity Village MO, 1949], 83). The Divine Idea emerges from the One Divine Mind and is interpreted by us, collectively and individually.

Spiritually, our word and our thought are interchangeable. Whether our word and thought is spiritual or "only human" depends upon our understanding and perception in the moment. Although the Divine Idea is true, our "only human" filter may limit our recognition of the Divine Idea. Our human idea may appear very different from the Divine Idea, but even so, our words and thoughts are powerful.

The words we speak and the thoughts we think reveal our beliefs and expectations. Words form impressions and have effects. Whether spoken aloud or internally, whether formed from the alphabet or felt as emotions, words declare what is and what will be, from the point of present understanding. Here is an example:

A woman new to town approached her neighbor, who was relaxing on his front porch. After exchanging hellos, the newcomer asked, "What are people like in this town?"

The friendly neighbor responded with a question of his own. "What were people like in the town you used to live in?"

"Oh dear." The woman hesitated. "My family and I could hardly wait to get out of that town. Everyone was unkind and distrustful."

The man on his porch shook his head from side to side while remarking, "Well, you will find that people are that way here as well."

On another day, another family moving to the same neighborhood said hello to the man rocking in his chair on his porch. The woman asked, "What are people like in this town?"

The neighbor asked back, "What were they like in the town you used to live in?"

The woman replied, "We were sad to leave our home, because people in that town were wonderful, kind, and caring."

The man on his porch nodded his head in agreement and said, "Well, you will find that people are that way here as well."

The newcomers' beliefs and expectations had the power to shape their experiences. Likewise, the power of the Word is revealing, formative, and creative. Just as the beliefs and language of the women in the story will shape their future experiences, so our words in prayer shape ours.

Words Are Revealing

Words reveal to us our innermost beliefs and expectations. Words reveal the quality of our consciousness. Words are the keys to the heart. What we believe about ourselves, others, and the world comes out of our mouths. Our words teach us about our present unconscious assumptions. What we believe also returns to us as feedback from the world. New Thought mystic Neville Goddard taught, "Think of the world as a sounding box, echoing and reflecting what you have assumed." ("The Incarnate Revelation" [lecture, February 20, 1969], *www.nevillelecturehall.com/neville-lecture89.html*).

Words Are Formative

Words produce effects. Whether our words and thoughts spring from our own experience or from our interpretation of others' words, what we tell ourselves affects us.

Throughout my preteen and teen years, I was bombarded with messages about my body shape, which I internalized. My two older brothers called me names like Hippo Hips and Thunder Thighs. My female relatives, including my mother, reminded me time and time again that I had received the double whammy; that is, I was destined to have the shape of my female Italian peasant ancestors from both sides of the family. I felt enormous and self-conscious about it. Years later, paging through my photo album with my daughter, who by then was a teenager, I felt startled to see that I had looked lovely as a young woman.

The formative power of the word is in its effect. The effect on me as a teenager was that I saw myself as a real-life version of the words spoken about me. Words (and thoughts) affect our bodies' health and sense of well-being. Words of encouragement, worthiness, and optimism build our bodies' immune systems, whereas words of discouragement, unworthiness, and pessimism inhibit our bodies' immune systems.

Naturally, the question arises: must we worry about every fleeting word? Many New Thought teachers caution us to watch our every thought, in keeping with a narrow understanding of the power of the Word. Be careful, they warn, because every thought and every word produces.

I, for one, do not subscribe to the idea that every spur-of-the-moment, passing thought brings into fruition the literal equivalent of the thought. If this were the case, nearly every person would be a murderer several times over. How many times as a child did you wish the worst on someone—parent, teacher, babysitter, or friend? Weren't you relieved to know your angry thoughts did not result in harm?

"All words [thoughts] are formative, but not all words [thoughts] are creative," Charles Fillmore wrote. (*The Revealing Word*, 178). Only our dominant, persistent thought, backed up by powerful feeling, bursts open like a germinating seed and pushes up above ground to bring forth blossoms that produce more seeds just like it. Henry David Thoreau said it like this:

> As a single footstep will not make a path on the earth,
> so a single thought will not make a pathway in the mind.
> To make a deep physical path, we walk again and again.
> To make a deep mental path, we must think over and
> over the kind of thoughts we wish to dominate our lives.

Words Are Creative

Words and thoughts that are creative are those we dwell upon. We dwell upon words and thoughts that prompt strong feelings and potent images—like the words *hippo hips* and *thunder thighs* did for me as a teenager. I look back at the photographs of my teen body with regret that I did not appreciate my body at that time. I find today that the influence of those early messages lingers, and I still easily see through warped, outdated lenses reflecting a tainted body image. However, I now also notice that my conscious thoughts of well-being produce an image of wholeness, goodness, and beauty. Either way I see myself in a given moment, I choose the consequential experience.

The creative capacity of the Word likens the Word to a seed. When a seed is planted in fertile soil, and nurtured, it germinates and grows. Its growth is predictable, isn't it? A marigold seed will only produce a marigold plant, and a peach seed will never eventuate in a cherry tree. What we think and say are like seeds producing comparable thoughts and words. The creative Word produces its kind, faithfully reflecting the nature of the seed-word.

Have you ever opened a packet of wildflower seeds and sown them in your garden? Have you noticed that the blossoming garden bears little resemblance to the photograph on the seed packet? The packet promises a variety of beautiful wildflower blossoms, but in your garden only one or two of the varieties flourish. We may not be delighted with these results in a flower garden, but we can be glad our consciousness does not bring into bloom every word and every thought casually tossed there.

Thoughts and words that blossom have taken root in fertile mind-soil. They have been cultivated, tended to. They produce in abundance, creating more of the same. Thoughts and words that have not been nurtured are not creative. They have not stuck, for they have not prompted strong feelings or hysterical imaginings.

In our early years of marriage, my husband, Giles, was stationed at an air force base. By the time our son had turned two and our daughter had been born, Giles frequently deployed on military business. Our house was located near one of the entrances to the base, where gate guards checked for valid identification before authorizing access to the base. I should have felt safe on the base.

A new mother, however, I fretted about negative possibilities that had never occurred to me before I had babies. I became a light sleeper, listening for any sign I was needed by my little ones during the night. When Giles was away, I could not fall asleep at all for worrying about the horrible things that could happen. I imagined that if someone broke into our house intending to harm me, I would not have time to reach my children's rooms before this someone would reach me. I began walking through my house at night, imagining various scenarios, including how to get out onto the roof and how to attack back if I were surprised in my room during the night. I found a metal pipe in someone's trash and stashed it under my bed. I tried to imagine myself using it but realized I could not pop someone over the head with the pipe, so I visualized having a gun.

I could not buy a gun. I could not imagine myself aiming and pulling the trigger even to save myself.

Throughout this time, I worried about something else. Having been a student of spirituality, having learned that thoughts have effects, I worried that my fearful thoughts would bring about the very thing I feared. I rationalized, then, that I had to be even *more* vigilant than before. I became frenzied: one night lying awake until dawn, the next sleeping fitfully in sheer exhaustion.

Eventually, I decided to ask for support. The military police officers were happy to walk through my house with me, suggesting ways to improve upon my family's security. I followed their suggestion to talk to our neighbors. Our neighbors' house was attached to ours. From our bedroom I could hear their clothes hangers scratching along the bar in their closet next door. My neighbors agreed to respond if I were to rap three times on the wall of my bedroom during the night.

Most important, I stopped feeding my hysterical imagination. I turned to the principles and practices that had sustained me while in residence at the ashram. I recognized that the fearful thoughts were temporary, certainly not akin to my nature or my experience. I consciously changed my words, my thoughts, and my outlook. I began sleeping well again at night.

We are not forever stuck with our first words, or thoughts, on any subject. When we pay attention to our words, we are empowered to choose them, claim them, and live out from them. In *Conversations with God: An Uncommon Dialogue* (book 1 [New York: G. P. Putnam's Sons, 1995], 93), Neale Donald Walsch wrote, "When you catch yourself thinking negative thoughts—thoughts that negate your highest idea about a thing—think again!"

Precisely. This is the purpose of affirmative prayer, to think again, to speak another word, an empowering word.

Update Your Words in Prayer

The words we speak and the thoughts we think can be revealing, formative, and creative. True. However, our words and thoughts all spring from *the* Word, the originating Divine Idea. As such, we are capable of hearing the Word unfiltered by human feelings or experience. Affirmative prayer is the practice of recognizing the Word of truth. Affirmative prayer is the practice of realizing, affirming, and then being the living Word.

This is the purpose of affirmative prayer, to think again, to speak another word, an empowering word.

Here is a practical approach to affirmative prayer that is compatible with an evolving understanding of GOD (Divine Nature) and the Power of the Word. Instead of talking to God, we acknowledge Divine Nature and our Divine Identity, knowing Oneness. Instead of asking God to change us, other people, or our conditions, we affirm the highest truth revealed in the moment. Instead of saying thank you to God, we feel and express appreciation in many other ways.

Acknowledge Divine Nature

A common practice at the start of prayer is reciting an invocation, traditionally a way of addressing God or asking God to be with us. For example, *Father, we call upon you during this time* or *Praise you, God, for your mercy and grace.*

In affirmative prayer, *invoking* is calling to mind, or bringing into awareness, the divine. The word *invoke* originates from the

Latin *invocare* meaning "in" plus "voice." The meaning closest to the Latin is "to conjure" or "to bring forth from within." Affirmative prayer is the practice of realizing the nature of the divine that, in truth, is the "within" of you. Affirmative prayer is realizing Divine Consciousness at the moment you become conscious of the truth. As you become convinced of your Divine Identity, you take on that identity in prayer.

As you read the following prayers of invocation, the original words of Charles Fillmore as well as Paul Hasselbeck's adaptation that follows, notice how you respond energetically and emotionally to each.

I am now in the presence of Pure Being
Immersed in the Holy Spirit of Life, Love, and Wisdom.
I acknowledge Thy presence and power, O blessed Spirit.
In Thy Divine Wisdom now erase my mortal limitations.
From Thy pure substance of Love bring into manifestation my
* world according to Thy perfect law.*

I AM the presence of Pure Being
Emanating the Holy Spirit of Life, Love, and Wisdom.
I AM all that GOD is expressing at the point of me.
As I express Divine Wisdom,
All thoughts of mortal limitation have no power over me.
I AM the substance and power of pure Love
Bringing into manifestation my world according to divine law.

Notice the language changes from the first example to the second. In the first, we presume separation when adopting phrases such as "I am now in the presence." As our understanding of Divine Nature has evolved, we can no longer say we are that without feeling separate from Divine Nature. As the second example shows, we actually acknowledge "I AM the presence" to the degree and at the point of our present understanding. Likewise, in the first example, Divine Nature is addressed as a person. This is not so in the second example, in which we assert our Divine Identity.

Acknowledging Divine Nature by use of words is a personal matter. We select words that authentically reflect our understanding and resonate emotionally. The word *God* is well-worn, defined in the English language as a male deity, and rife with doctrinal associations. We benefit from asking ourselves, *What do I know about Divine Nature?*

The word *God* is well-worn, defined in the English language as a male deity, and rife with doctrinal associations. We benefit from asking ourselves, *What do I know about Divine Nature?*

Some of my favorite expressions that acknowledge Divine Nature, and thereby my Divine Identity, are these:

- All That Is, I AM.

- Infinite Love is my name and nature.

- Oneness is all I see.

- Only GOD, Only Good.

- I AM Divine Life, Love, and Wisdom.

For a prayer at the beginning of a gathering, most of us have learned a basic formula something like this:

Dear God, thank you for bringing us together today for the purpose of accomplishing this assignment. We ask your guidance and grace so that your work may be done through us. May we all be blessed by this activity, and may others be blessed by us. Thank you, God. Amen.

Many times groups are eager to get past the prayer and to the work ahead. Group leaders often say, "Let's quickly pray and get started." Prayer can become perfunctory, hurried, and meaningless. It becomes little more than a required agenda item. More concerning, the energy generated by this kind of prayer is all in the head. It appeals to *doing* rather than *being*.

A different gathering can emerge—a gathering of energy—if it is spawned by a powerful acknowledgement of Divine Nature and the Divine Identity of all. Here are three examples of statements with which we might begin this type of gathering:

We pause in our day to breathe deeply and enter into a greater awareness of Divine Life that we are. Individual though we appear, we are One in Divine Life, with One powerful intention stemming from One Mind.

In this moment of awareness, we recognize Infinite Love is the magnet that draws us together. We are expressing from Divine Love as a unity of purpose.

We take the time right now to remember All That Is, I AM. Breathing into this awareness, we know ourselves as expansive, purposeful, and divine.

What do you notice as you read these invocations compared with those you have heard in the past? Notice the feelings that arise as you assert Divine Nature. Do you feel empowered? Can you imagine the continuity of the group gathered in agreement with these truths? As we grow in our understanding, we become capable of naturally expressing the words of invocation that ratify our Divine Identity and raise us to the awareness of All That Is.

Affirm the Highest Truth Revealed in the Moment

When contemplating Divine Nature and identifying ourselves as divine, we are destined to believe, as Macrina Wiederkehr wrote, "the truth about [ourselves], no matter how beautiful it is" (quoted in *A Grateful Heart* edited by M. J. Ryan). Over time, we raise our opinion of ourselves. We agree with our Divine Nature. We come to realize the truth about ourselves and life itself as revealed in prayer.

One Sunday morning, very early before the sun rose, I sniffed in a few sprays of saline solution in the kitchen. I dropped the tiny top to the bottle. Not fully awake and not yet thinking clearly, I crawled around on my hands and knees for the longest time, asking my hands to see what my eyes could not. All around the kitchen I scooted, with no luck. Finally I stood up and turned on the light, and the little lid was easy to spot.

Truth revealed is akin to turning the light on and discovering the saline spray bottle cap was there all the time. Truth is truth whether we realize it or not. But truth realized awakens us to live as the Divine Light we are.

When I feel worried about my life, fearful or depressed, what truth might come into my awareness in a time of prayer? Perhaps this is the truth about my life: I am not a bundle of nervous energy or a dim bulb. *I AM the visible expression of the great invisible All, the Light of the World.* The new "Dear God" is "What truth is being revealed in this moment?"

When I am concerned about my health, here is the truth coming into my awareness: Even if my physical body is not well, I can assert my Divine Identity. *I AM Divine Life. Wholeness and wellness are my True Nature.*

The new "Dear God" is "What truth is being revealed in this moment?"

During a time of friction in a relationship, this truth may be revealed: My nature is not dysfunctional, bitter, or unforgiving. *I AM an expression of Divine Love, an extension of divine compassion. I AM the magnetizing, harmonizing, unifying power of Divine Love.*

Pondering my purpose, I realize through prayer, I am not a random happening or a meaningless human life. *I AM the Power of Intention expressing in my truest thoughts, words, and actions. My Divine Life serves the world.*

When questioning my worth, this truth reassures me: Everything that is makes a valuable contribution to the whole. *I AM; therefore I am valuable. I AM a Divine Gift given to the world. I am here to embody the Word. I am here to be the light of the world!*

Express Appreciation

My sister-in-law Ann has reason to feel appreciation every day, she says. Every morning upon awakening, Ann concentrates her attention on her fingers and toes. If she can wiggle her fingers and toes, and then move her limbs, she feels just about giddy with enthusiasm. You see, Ann lives with multiple sclerosis. For months at a time she is symptom-free, and then, without warning, she is unable to walk without assistance. Every day is precious. Ann knows this.

Appreciation is good for all of us. Our body temples respond to appreciation by manufacturing chemicals that heighten feelings of well-being. Spiritually, appreciation *appreciates*. Put another way, what we appreciate increases in value. The image of appreciation is hands open wide, the position of receiving. In his book *Prosperity*, Charles Fillmore teaches, "Praise and thanksgiving impart the quickening spiritual power that produces growth and increase in all things" (Unity Books: Unity Village MO, 1995), 65).

In prayer, it is customary to express appreciation. Traditionally, words of thanksgiving are addressed to God, as if God were human. "Thank you, God," or some variation, is probably spoken more often in prayer than any other phrase is ever spoken on the planet. Yet, as our understanding of Divine Nature evolves, talking to God seems disingenuous. Expressing appreciation, however, remains essential.

My son, Adrian, was the first to awaken one Christmas morning when he was a preteen. My husband, Giles, and I felt joyous anticipation knowing that Adrian's gift was just what he had asked for, a huge boom box. Too large to fit under the Christmas tree, the gift was covered with a colorful cloth on a table. The moment Adrian entered the living room, he knew that giant package belonged to him. As he pulled off the cloth with his left hand, Adrian's right hand shot up straight toward the ceiling. He lifted his head, opened his mouth, and let out the loudest "Yes!" I have ever heard. Adrian oozed appreciation.

There are as many ways of expressing appreciation as there are people and as there are reasons to appreciate. In prayer, we can appreciate our capacity to awaken to expansive truth. We can express delight in new understanding or in feelings of peace. We can shout out "hooray!" or "Amen!" We can laugh out loud. We can squeeze the hands holding ours. As one of my colleagues does, we can even turn to those around us and say to each of them, "Thank you, GOD." Or we can sit silently in awe.

Sample Affirmative Prayers

With practice, you can experience a greater sense of Oneness than you have when you talked to GOD in prayer. You can authentically express words that heal, uplift, and strengthen yourself and others. Here are three examples:

I turn within, shifting my awareness from the world around me to the Life I AM, breathing the breath of Divine Life. Right where I am is All That Is. Right where I am is all the vitality I could ever need. I cannot run out of energy, for I AM divine. Divine Energy can never run out, because Divine Energy flows from Divine Life. I celebrate today, living fully and freely, gratefully, for I AM Divine Life.

I look to the beauty of All That Is around me and All That Is within me, and all that I AM. Everywhere I look, I behold wondrous Divine Order. I know the sun rises every morning, even when I cannot see it for the clouds that cover its shining. I too am Divine Order. The Light I

AM is always shining, even when clouded thinking obscures my view. I shine brightly today, joyfully observing Divine Order in everything and everyone.

In this moment, I rise to the high mountain of spiritual awareness, where the view is vast and without obstruction. Here I am in the Kingdom of the Heavens, a consciousness of Divine Clarity. Divine Clarity makes molehills out of my mountains of worry. Where before I was an "only human" captivated by fearful imaginings, now I AM Divine Clarity captivated by a view of magnificent possibilities. The picture from this perspective is clear. I appreciate my clear vision and delight in expectation of Good.

Reform the Words of Traditional Prayers

Practice of affirmative prayer over time may lead you to rethink prayers, hymns, and recitations that for years you had not questioned. Now that you consciously select prayer language congruent with an evolving consciousness, you may feel dissatisfied with religious language that at one time felt comforting.

In my spiritual community, affirmative language is taught and practiced. Once, in a prayer class, I played a recording of a popular contemporary Christian song, "Holiness" by Scott Underwood. I chose this song intentionally, to stimulate my students' feelings

> Nothing is more humbling than to be Divine Nature expressing at the point of our individuality. From this perspective, our Divine Life is awe-inspiring.

regarding prayer language. They heard this appeal to God: "Brokenness is what I long for, brokenness is what I need, brokenness is what You want from me." Perhaps at one time, the idea of being a broken human appealing to a divine superhuman gave you comfort. I assure you this was not the case for my students. Their responses revealed surprise about the degradation of Divine Identity implied in the lyrics. Emotionally, students felt smaller, disempowered, and disconnected—likely not the intention of the songwriter.

Prayer language presupposing a chasm between GOD and humanity belies the truth of our Divine Identity. It brings to mind a standardized prayer in the Catholic Mass, intended to increase humility and receptivity to God: "Oh, Lord, I am not worthy to receive You, but only say the word and I shall be healed." As we have grown in spiritual understanding, we realize that the speaker of the Word is GOD, not God separate from us but GOD I AM. I speak the Word. I declare the Oneness of Divine Nature that I AM. In my "only human" thinking, I can feel separate from GOD; therefore, I heal my "only human" thinking by speaking words of Oneness arising from spiritual understanding. Our spiritual understanding of these words does not diminish GOD. On the contrary, it amplifies the amazing reality of Divine Nature and our Divine Identity. Nothing is more humbling than to be Divine Nature expressing at the point of our individuality. From this perspective, our Divine Life is awe-inspiring.

By means of our growing spiritual understanding, we can reform the language of prayer. We can reinterpret classic prayers, assigning to them meaning that is congruent with our evolving consciousness of oneness. Here are some examples of invocations at the start of prayers in various traditions, followed by my up-dated language of affirmative prayer:

Our Father which art in heaven; hallowed be Thy name.

(Christianity)

The Source of All That Is, Divine Light, exists in and through everything. It is my sacred nature.

O Allah, I supplicate you to grant me your Love.

(Islam)

I AM Divine Love springing from the One Creative Power.

Creator, hear us, for we are your children. Father, we thank you for all that you have given us.

(Native American)

One Creative Power is the Source of all. All That the Source is, I AM at the point of my awareness. I celebrate my Divine Identity.

In the same way, we can relanguage entire prayers from fa-miliar faith traditions, deepening understanding and increasing resonance. Here are some examples:

The Lord's Prayer

The most recited prayer in Christianity, the Lord's Prayer is trans-lated and interpreted from the teaching of Jesus as recorded in the Gospels of Matthew and Luke. Jesus was asked by his disciples, "How shall we pray?" Jesus replied, "In this way," after which he recited heartfelt words rich with metaphoric language that resonated with his listeners. Jesus was not instructing his disciples to say those words exactly, but to pray in that manner. Read the following lines of the Lord's Prayer, or recite it as it is familiar to you.

Our Father which art in heaven
Hallowed be Thy name
Thy kingdom come, Thy will be done
On earth as it is in heaven
Give us this day our daily bread
And forgive us our debts [trespasses]
As we have forgiven our debtors [those who have trespassed
    against us]
And leave us not in temptation [lead us not into temptation]
But deliver us from evil
For Thine is the kingdom, the power, and the glory forever
Amen.

The familiar words of the Lord's Prayer in English are far removed from the original words in the original language spoken by Jesus. Aramaic and Bible scholar Dr. Rocco Errico recommends the following text as a translation closest in meaning to the words purported to have been spoken by Jesus millennia ago (from *Setting a Trap for God: The Aramaic Prayer of Jesus* by Rocco Errico [Unity Books, Unity School of Christianity, 1997]).

Our Father who is everywhere,
Let Your name be set apart.
Come Your kingdom [counsel].
Let Your desire be, as in the universe, also on the earth.
Provide us our needful bread from day to day.

And free us from our offenses, as also we have freed our offenders.
And do not let us enter into temptation, but separate us from error.
For belongs to You the kingdom, the power, and the song and praise,
From all ages throughout all ages.
[Sealed in trust, truth, and faithfulness.]

Another Aramaic and Bible scholar, Dr. Neil Douglas-Klotz, translated the ancient Aramaic version of the New Testament mystically, metaphorically, and poetically. According to Douglas-Klotz, the following translation is one of many possible translations, because ancient Aramaic words and phrases contained multiple meanings in various contexts. As you read Douglas-Klotz's translation, relate each of its lines to the lines of the prayer familiar to you.

O Birther! Father-Mother of the Cosmos
Focus your light within us—make it useful.
Create your reign of unity now
Through our fiery hearts and willing hands
Help us love beyond our ideals
And sprout acts of compassion for all creatures.
Animate the earth within us: we then
Feel the Wisdom underneath supporting all.
Untangle the knots within
So that we can mend our hearts' simple ties to each other.
Don't let surface things delude us
But free us from what holds us back from our true purpose.
Out of you, the astonishing fire,
Returning light and sound to the cosmos.
Amen.

Inspired by Douglas-Klotz's work and my study of Unity metaphysics, I have reformed the language of The Lord's Prayer for myself. These words ring with truth as I know it, opening me to the reality of Divine Nature and my Divine Identity.

Light of the world shines within me, outside me, all around me.
Looking to the Light, I am led by the Light.
I reflect the Light in my innermost thoughts
As well as my outermost actions.
Every day every good comes my way.
The Light I AM keeps me from being caught up in superficial or
material matters.
I am freed from being out of rhythm with my Divine Identity.
From the One Source comes the vision, the energy to bring forth
the vision, and the harmony of this manifested vision with
all of creation.
This is the foundation from which I take my next step.

Reread these versions of the Lord's Prayer with attention to your feelings as you relate to each statement. Feel your way to language that awakens you, shakes you up, or soothes you. Rewrite the Lord's Prayer in your own words, words that reveal truth as you know it.

Prayer for Protection

James Dillet Freeman's Prayer for Protection has provided spiritual confidence and comfort to millions of people through the past century. The prayer was written by Freeman for all soldiers during

World War II, many of whom carried the prayer in their uniform pockets. The prayer was taken to the moon by Apollo Astronaut Edwin "Buzz" Aldrin in 1969. It has been whispered by people in hospital beds, at take-off on airplanes, and at times of uncertainty. The original prayer contained twelve lines but is best known as this shorter version:

> *The light of God surrounds me*
> *The love of God enfolds me*
> *The power of God protects me*
> *The presence of God watches over me*
> *Wherever I Am, God is.*

At the close of many New Thought church services, the Prayer for Protection is recited, usually in plural form. In my spiritual community, we have updated the language as follows:

> *We are here to glow as the Light of* GOD. *We are the Light of* GOD.
> *We are here to embrace as the love of* GOD. *We are the Love of* GOD.
> *We are here to stand in Truth as the Power of* GOD. *We are the Power of* GOD.
> *We are here to radiate as the Presence of* GOD. *We are the Presence of* GOD.
> *Wherever we are,* GOD *is. And so it is!*

Reading these versions of the prayer, feel your way to words that synchronize with your spiritual understanding and empower you to live into your Divine Identity.

The Knots Prayer

The contemporary prayer referred to as the Knots Prayer and attributed to an anonymous source has gained popularity over the Internet. It is easy to see why. The prayer is evocative of human struggle with will and worth. However, the prayer is supplicatory rather than affirmative.

Dear God:

Please untie the knots that are in my mind, my heart, and my life.

Remove the have nots, the can nots, and the do nots that I have in my mind

Erase the will nots, may nots, might nots that may find a home in my heart.

Release me from the could nots, would nots, and should nots that obstruct my life.

And most of all, dear God, I ask that you remove from my mind, my heart, and my life all the "am nots" that I have allowed to hold me back, especially the thought that I am not good enough.

Amen.

This prayer provides us a particularly fitting example of how *not* to pray affirmatively! Read my version in comparison and notice how you feel about yourself as you review both versions.

I breathe deeply into this moment of high awareness, One with All That Is.

I AM the power of Release, untying the knots in my mind, my heart, and my life.

I AM Divine Love in harmony with others and myself.

I AM the power of Will, willingly releasing the thought of
    have not and cannot.
I AM Divine Mind, abundant and capable.
I AM the power of Imagination dissolving the energy of will not,
    may not, and might not, could not, would not, and should
    not.
I AM Divine Wisdom knowing all things are possible.
I AM the power of Life, claiming my vibrancy, vitality, and
    value. I celebrate my True Nature, which is divine.

Now that we have reformed our language in prayer, we have built a powerful basis for the practice of affirmative prayer. Next we will study the principles of denial and affirmation in prayer.

Talk to Yourself

- Write or speak of a time you experienced the power of words (thoughts).

- If you no longer address God to begin a time of prayer, how might you establish yourself in the consciousness of GOD at the start of prayer? Write your own invocation.

- Recall a time you prayed when you were worried or uncertain. What language did your prayer consist of? How might you pray differently now, knowing more about affirmative prayer?

- Reread and reflect upon the various versions of prayers in this chapter. Journal or converse with others about your reflections. When you recite these words, which versions spark feelings of confidence, empowerment, and reassurance? Explain why.

Chapter 4

Practice Denials and Affirmations in Prayer

Denial erases, dissolves, and releases. Affirmation claims, plants, and builds.

—*Sharon Connors,* Adventures in Prayer: Praying Your Way to a God You Can Trust *(2004)*

Learn the language of denying and affirming that is believable to body, mind, and spirit. Practice denials and affirmations in prayer.

Much of what we believe we have unintentionally acquired, unknowingly held, and unconsciously enacted. This is especially true of limiting or negative beliefs, because they are backed by strong emotion.

If you grew up in a household struggling to make ends meet, you may have overheard adults discussing the poor economy and threats of layoffs. You may have listened as they questioned, *How will we ever be able to send our kids to college?* When you asked to buy a new outfit for the school dance, the response might have been, *What's wrong with the outfit you wore to the last dance? Money doesn't grow on trees, you know.* When the threatened layoff happened, you may have overheard your discouraged parent saying, *I don't know how we're supposed to get ahead in this world.*

As important, you probably *felt* your parents' suffering as they strove to meet the household's financial demands. Perhaps at times you said to yourself, *When I grow up I will always have enough money.* Even if you have enough money as an adult, you may have unintentionally acquired, unknowingly held, and unconsciously enacted *there is never enough.*

We determine our experience moment by moment, by our choice of thought. We decide what is possible and what is not. Mostly, we do this unconsciously, through a well-developed habit of thought that over time solidifies into belief. Unconscious though they may be, beliefs about what is possible and what is not limit our expectations, leading to impaired vision. With impaired vision, we cannot see that we determine our experience moment by moment. Instead, we resort to wishing and beseeching in everything, including in prayer. All the while our choice of thought determines our experience. In prayer, we can consciously choose our thought in practice of denial and affirmation. By this practice, we correct impaired vision and realize truth.

Denial

One day my kitchen sink clogged. The garbage disposal became useless. I thought if I added something coarse to the drain, whatever was stuck would loosen and the watery material collecting in the sink would drain. I emptied a bucket of ice cubes from the freezer. The water level rose. I cut up a few lemons. Lemon soup. Nothing added would allow the sink to drain. Eventually I realized I would have to remove the blockage by pulling it out, not pushing it through, in order to clear the drain. When our minds are congested with unconscious assumptions and limiting beliefs, repeating affirmations is like adding ice cubes and lemons to a clogged sink.

First, we must clear away the mental congestion. This is the value of denial. Spiritual denial, also called release or renunciation, is dis-identification with, repudiation of, and elimination of thoughts and beliefs that we realize are contrary to spiritual Truth.

I like to think of denial as spiritual Ex-Lax. In the human body, if waste cannot move through, toxicity sets in. The body is designed for release, but a buildup of stress and poor eating habits leads to constipation. Relief from acute constipation is often found in medicine that prompts elimination.

> Spiritual denial is dis-identification with, renunciation of, and elimination of thoughts and beliefs that we realize are contrary to spiritual Truth.

Understanding the spiritual power of denial is like having a ready-made laxative for cases of spiritual constipation.

Denial Is Not for Facts or Feelings

A joke: A student of New Thought died and became aware he had landed in hell. Exercising denial, he repeated, "It's not hot, and I'm not here!"

Let's be clear. Spiritual denial is different from psychological denial. Denial in psychology is refusal to face facts and avoidance of feelings. Psychological denial leads to self-delusion as well as unconscious action and inaction.

In the practice of spiritual denial, we do not deny facts or feelings! We do not pretend our feelings and circumstances away. We do not deny pain, whether physical or emotional. We do not try to convince ourselves that *this* is not happening.

Feelings must be dealt with in the practice of denial, even as feelings are not to be denied. Feelings arise as indicators of belief. For example, if I believe *there is not enough*, naturally I feel vulnerable or anxious. I do not deny feeling vulnerable or anxious, but I deny these feelings a resting place in my consciousness. I deny their importance and power. I let them pass through. Rather than deny feelings, I deal directly with the false belief formed in my consciousness.

The true power of spiritual denial occurs when we comprehend the falsehood of our *assumptions* about facts and feelings. We notice that facts and feelings are fleeting; they change moment to moment. We observe that our feelings shift as we reinterpret the meaning of facts. Spiritual denial leads to awareness of our Divine Identity, feelings of relief, and conscious action. True denial corrects consciousness. True denial erases belief in "only human" consciousness.

Around the time of her fortieth birthday, my friend Marjorie was dining at her favorite restaurant. Several tables away, in the designated smoking section, another patron lit a cigarette. The cigarette smoke made a beeline to Marjorie's nostrils. The smoker might as well have been sitting at Marjorie's table blowing smoke directly into her face. Unexpectedly, Marjorie's lungs constricted. Without warning, for the first time in her life, she began wheezing.

True denial corrects consciousness. True denial erases belief in "only human" consciousness.

Marjorie was diagnosed with asthma. She, who had never suffered ill health, felt stunned by this news. She refused medication, preferring to ignore the persistent symptoms. When experiencing shortness of breath, Marjorie would tell herself, "I do not have asthma! I am healthy."

After several weeks, Marjorie relented. She began a course of medical treatment to relieve acute symptoms. Telling her mother the news, Marjorie was reminded that her mother had developed asthma around the same age.

Marjorie, a student of New Thought spirituality, struggled with this new fact of her life. If asthma could arise out of nowhere to threaten her heath, Marjorie feared that other dangers also might be looming. Marjorie worried that her vehement opposition to public smoking had attracted to her the very thing she had most feared. Moreover, she became uncomfortably aware of the difference between the spiritual principles she espoused and the seeming reality of her newly diagnosed condition. Denying the condition had not made it go away. Accepting the condition appeared an act of unfaithfulness to her stated beliefs.

Marjorie's spiritual struggle is familiar; from time to time, each of us faces human conditions that challenge our spiritual understanding. When we misapply the powerful tool of spiritual denial, we confuse ourselves into believing this spiritual tool isn't working.

Deny Untruth

If we do not deny facts or feelings, what do we deny? We deny thoughts and beliefs counter to spiritual truth. We deny belief in the permanence of facts and feelings. We deny negative interpretations of the circumstances. We deny identification with the condition. We deny misguided beliefs about Divine Nature and our Divine Identity.

Deny Belief in the Permanence of Facts and Feelings

"Nothing endures but change," a truism Greek philosopher Heraclitus coined in the 4th century BC, rings false when we are in the midst of a compelling human condition. When facts grab our attention, giving rise to potent feelings about them, nothing else exists for us in that moment. We become mesmerized by the intensity of the situation, seemingly unable to imagine a time before or the possibility of a future without the condition.

Despite their seeming reality, facts change. One day a medical test points to a tumor. A repeat scan, a few weeks later, reveals no tumor precisely where there had been one in the first test's results.

One day Marjorie breathes easily. The next day, her breathing becomes labored.

Spiritual denial is a prayer practice that snaps us out of the trance of permanence. Upon examination, from our own experience, we can point to countless situations proving that facts, and feelings, change.

Check it out: You stub your toe. You feel pain. The toe heals. Pain goes away. Or your loved one dies. You feel grief. Your loved one appears to you in a dream. You feel peaceful.

Marjorie's air passages became inflamed. She felt afraid. She could point to a time, moments before, when she had breathed easily and felt well. She could remind herself that as suddenly as asthma appeared, it could disappear. She could soothe herself, relieving fear and thereby supporting life, by these words of denial: *I refuse to dwell upon asthma or give it any importance. I give no power to a fleeting condition.*

Deny Negative Interpretations of Circumstances

We make up all sorts of nonsensical reasons why things happen, mostly incriminating ourselves and one another by associating unwanted conditions with past behaviors. We have caused the car to be stolen by harboring fearful thoughts. Our friend betrayed us because we had spoken unkindly about her years ago. Marjorie got asthma as punishment for condemning smokers.

Self-reflection can be illuminating, leading to self-realization and useful transformation of thought. However, when we are in the middle of a challenging circumstance, self-reflection is prone to slip into self-condemnation. Focused on what we thought, said, or did wrong, we bind ourselves to the unwanted condition. Denial of negative interpretations and their seeming power removes condemnation.

Denial of negative interpretations could be stated this way: *I do not indulge in self-accusation. I deny the relevance and influence of misguided thoughts. I deny the idea that I deserve to suffer as punishment for unenlightened thoughts, words, or actions. In truth, there is no condemnation.*

Deny Identification with the Condition

The more intense the condition, the more easily it consumes our attention. Over time, we can mistake our condition for our identity. Language such as "my diabetes" and excuses such as "this is all I can expect, in my condition" signify the condition has taken over my life.

My friend Patricia inspired me during her years of medical and spiritual treatment as she insisted that cancer did not define her. She proclaimed, essentially, *Symptoms of disease and side effects of medical treatment do not constitute my life!* When the time came for her body to die, Patricia went gently, unafraid, and certain that her Divine Life is as irrepressible as it is eternal.

These are some statements to deny identification with a condition: *The origin of my life is not my body or my circumstances. I am not my conditions. Nothing can take over my Divine Identity. No temporary condition could possibly define me or limit the fullness of my Divine Life.*

Deny Compliance with Collective Consciousness

Business leaders know the danger of groupthink among boards and task teams. Groupthink is mindless conformity, neglecting to question the majority thought and behavior. When groupthink is operating, the team is most likely to miss a critical possibility leading toward success or away from failure.

Collective consciousness, or mass consciousness, is macrocosmic groupthink; it is a limitation that easily leads to short-sightedness. In the collective consciousness, ideas exist that *everyone* believes are true, whether explicitly or implicitly. Examples: some illnesses are incurable; pollens cause seasonal allergies; disease is inevitable; times are tough; jobs are scarce.

Before the year 1885, prevailing thought held that climbing Mount Everest was impossible. In his book *Above the Snow Line* published that same year, Clinton Thomas Dent proposed otherwise. Since then, more than fourteen hundred daring individuals have ventured upward to prove Dent right and change the commonly held belief about Mount Everest.

Spiritual trailblazers are those who deny impossibility and refute seeming facts, forging ahead to prove that spiritual power supersedes "only human" power. Spiritual trailblazers show us what can *be*, can be—if we eliminate belief in limitation and impossibility.

Some statements to deny compliance with collective consciousness include these: *Nothing happening in the material world determines my financial well-being.*

What can *be, can be*—if we eliminate belief in limitation and impossibility.

No doctor, no scientist, no external authority could possibly predict the state of my health. I am not subject to the way of the world or the say of the world.

Deny Misguided Beliefs about Divine Nature and Our Divine Identity

Growing into our Divine Identity is a process that involves strengthening belief in our innate spiritual capacities. When circumstances appear daunting, we might wobble like a little girl attempting to walk in her mother's high heels. Each time we exercise denial of false beliefs, we strengthen our spiritual muscles and grow into our Divine Capacities.

There is no more urgent, crucial, or opportune time to deny misguided beliefs about our Divine Identity than when faced with daunting circumstances! During such times, it is imperative to use denials followed by affirmations to realize what it means to be divine. The Divine Nature is our standard; the truth is nothing less.

Marjorie, diagnosed with asthma, would practice denial with language such as this: *My identity is Divine; Divine Nature is never subject to damaging conditions. Asthma is not part of my Divine Life.*

We can proclaim in a similar way, and as Myrtle Fillmore did, when she wrote, "My True Nature is Divine Wholeness; I cannot inherit sickness."

What Good Could Come from Practicing Denial?

Perhaps you are thinking, practicing denial is well and good; however, we must still respond to our circumstances in some way.

Disclaiming false beliefs does not necessarily equate to an acceptable outcome. What good actually comes from exercising the power of denial?

When we remove falsehood, we stop fighting against facts and feelings. We stop blaming and condemning ourselves for these facts and feelings. We stop resisting our Divine Life. We stop viewing ourselves as "only human." We stop resigning ourselves to "only human" conditions. We stop subjecting ourselves to commonly held beliefs in lack and limitation. When we stop all this, we start to live in the clarity of our Divine Identity. Our actions spring from our Divine Identity. No longer mesmerized by human circumstance, no longer are we subject to the effects of human circumstance.

No longer mesmerized by human circumstance, no longer are we subject to the effects of human circumstance.

By persistently challenging false, limiting beliefs through denial, we get over our personal, myopic view of life; we claim, in truth, our expansive Divine Identity that contributes to the well-being of all. This is the good that comes from practicing denial.

How to Practice Denial (Release)

Constipation in the body is relieved by following a treatment plan. First, you ingest a purgative that rouses the organs of elimination. Second, you await the outcome in a supportive environment, however many hours it takes. Third, you sit on the pot, relax, and release. Finally, you flush.

Crude though this analogy may be, it is effective. Denial in prayer happens by means of a spiritual process akin to the biological process of elimination. First, you are provoked by a niggling realization that you are filled with false beliefs. Second, you heighten spiritual awareness through study, prayer, and meditation. Third, you cultivate a consciousness of denial by your words, leading to elimination of false beliefs. Finally, you flush—it is finished—with an emphatic *Amen!*

First: Provocation

You come to a point in consciousness when it seems you have taken a spiritual laxative. You become uncomfortably aware of how you have been blaming others for the bad things that have happened and blaming yourself for the good things that have not happened. You feel rumblings of shame, guilt, resentment, and excuses based upon false and limiting beliefs. You feel provoked by dissonance—the chasm between falsehoods you have believed to be true and truth itself. You know you have been off-truth, making stuff up. *Basta! Enough!*

Second: Heightened Spiritual Awareness

Heightened spiritual awareness is a fruit of study, prayer, and meditation. When practiced regularly, these disciplines prevent spiritual constipation. When we need a good spiritual purge, however, these disciplines become essential. They support us. They raise our awareness to the Truth that replaces falsehood.

This is the time to become steeped in truth. Optimally, go away for a few days in spiritual retreat. Here are some suggestions regardless of whether you physically go away or not:

- Turn off the television and radio.
- Refrain from caffeine and alcohol.
- Read the book that most inspires you.
- Chant while performing daily tasks—please not while driving.
- Invest more time in prayer and enlist a prayer partner for support.
- Engage in other practices that focus attention on the truth.

Third: Words of Denial

Words are important. Words reflect our understanding. Words of denial should be natural and unforced (like sitting on the pot is). For example, when you have been worrying incessantly about money, words of denial may flow this way:

While it seems natural for me to worry about money, worry is simply a feeling, and feelings come and go. I am not mesmerized by fleeting feelings. I am not and cannot be threatened by false notions of lack and limitation. I do not entertain fear of losing all that I have gained. I am not subject to the collective consciousness of fear and insecurity. I

do not participate in "ain't it awful" talk. I know money is
not my enemy.

Furthermore, I do not subscribe to belief in scarcity, as if
Divine Life could run out. I do not believe in a capricious
deity assigning wealth to some and poverty to others. I do not
believe that sudden unemployment or a decline in the value of
my investments happens as punishment for some unknown or
unconscious action on my part. My true value is not defined
by my present net worth.

Notice that effective words of denial are not vehement or
forced. They flow naturally, logically. Nonetheless, they are powerful in that they release pent-up falsehood. Intensity is reserved for
the affirmation that will follow.

Finally: Amen—It Is Finished

You have been successful in the practice of denial when your
thoughts, words, and actions no longer fixate on the false beliefs
you had unconsciously harbored. You have successfully eliminated
falsehood, flushing and washing your hands of the matter.

When I support others as they go through separation and di-
vorce, my role as a minister is to encourage a walk of grace and
integrity in the midst of pain and confusion. Often someone will
ask, "Will I always feel so stuck in anger, unable to go forward in
my life?" Yes, I am tempted to reply. Yes, you will feel this way until
you stop carrying her photo in your wallet, answering his text messages, or sleeping together one last time.

Actions such as these demonstrate false beliefs about relationships. A person behaving this way may believe he had only one chance at romance. She may confuse love with romantic fantasy. Furthermore, a person behaving this way confuses facts and feelings with truth. The fact is both partners have chosen to proceed independently of each other. Feelings rise and fall as on a roller coaster ride, varying from relief to panic and from rage to appreciation. The truth is, Divine Love cannot be interrupted, and no person is the source of that love.

You have been successful in the practice of denial when you no longer fixate on the false beliefs you had unconsciously harbored.

The flush following denial signifies ending and beginning again. We say *Amen*, the connotation of which is commonly understood as "The End." Amen also marks a beginning. The Aramaic word for *amen* can be translated as: "This is the foundation from which I proceed in truth."

An Example of Denial in Practice

All couples I know in long-standing romantic relationships go through good times and bad, richer and poorer, sickness and health. They also go through thrill and monotony, wrongly left out of traditional vows. Imagine yourself in a long-standing relationship, during a period of monotony. In your thoughts, you might say to your partner: *I have truckloads of evidence to support my premise that you and I are moving apart, going down separate paths. You don't bring me flowers anymore. You don't anticipate my every need. You don't read my mind. You don't do things my way. You don't wipe down the counter after using the kitchen. You don't gaze at me with romantic interest. You don't listen when I speak to you. I know this because you don't remember what I tell you.*

Your dissatisfaction appears irreparable. The more you replay this dialogue in your mind, with feeling, the truer and more irreparable it seems. Harboring such complaints about your partner, you suffer from a sense of separation, despair, and defeat to such a degree you consider ending the relationship.

You probably know you are viewing your experience from an "only human" perspective. No matter what you decide to do about your relationship, you are certain you want your actions to spring from your Divine Identity. Your feelings and thoughts about this circumstance are provocative. You are eager for relief.

Hungry for heightened spiritual awareness, you intensify your spiritual practice. You seek the truth and a way to authentically act in harmony with your Divine Identity. Out of the silence of spiritual practice arises your awareness of truth. Now you can clearly and authentically deny the false ideas and beliefs you had been harboring.

I deny the false notion that another person can cause me unhappiness. I do not derive my identity or my consciousness from my partner; I am not codependent in my relationship. I stop imagining the motivations behind my partner's actions, and I stop assuming my partner's actions spring from disinterest in me. I do not rely upon feelings of frustration and

insecurity as indicators about the state of my relationship. I
deny a belief that I could be separated from Divine Love in
which my partner
and I are united. I do not entertain thoughts that lower my
Divine Energy, shrinking my sense of self. I deny hysteri-
cal thinking a safe harbor in my consciousness. Divine Love,
my True Identity, can never be interrupted, fragmented, or
disconnected. I cannot lose the Love I AM.

Now that you know what is *not* true, you agree to refrain from entertaining such false ideas as you proceed to claim truth by practicing affirmation.

Practice Denial Regularly

Systems in body and being are living, which means they are in motion. Life is a continual stream of inflowing and outgoing. We would never expect once-in-a-lifetime physical elimination, knowing the body's health requires repeated inflowing nourishment and outgoing waste. We do not expect that the first time we clean our house will be the last time—though we wish it could be. Likewise, we recognize that we ingest massive amounts of information with byproducts such as erroneous ideas, misperceptions, and untruths. Our spiritual practice of denial acts as spiritual Ex-Lax, clearing consciousness.

Practice denial regularly. As a spiritual practice, repeatedly questioning your assumptions and releasing ideas contrary to truth prepares your consciousness for spiritual realization.

Affirmation

> Eloquent proclamations of spiritual Truth release the millions
> of electrons in our brain cells and through them blend like
> chords of mental music with the Mind universal.
>
> —*Charles Fillmore,* Atom-Smashing Power of Mind *(2010)*

An affirmation is a declaration of spiritual truth that, when we speak it, fixes our attention on truth. An affirmation supports us in the way an anchor holds a boat steady in its position on the water. An affirmation is a claim on truth, our demand on truth to establish itself in mind and heart. An affirmation rightfully follows a denial of a limiting or negative belief.

If you have ever replaced a lumpy mattress with a supportive one, you know that another night on the discarded mattress would be totally undesirable. An effective affirmation is like a supportive mattress. When truth awakens in consciousness, you cannot go back to a false belief without feeling uncomfortable.

Affirmation is a powerful spiritual practice. It is not merely positive thinking. Positive thinking is optimism, a worthy outlook to adopt. Positive thinking might offer a hopeful worldview but not a truth to uphold. Here are some examples of positive thoughts: "Every day in every way I am getting better and better." "It's all good." "Things have a way of turning out all right." Although such statements might help you feel more hopeful, they are not spiritual truths. Each of these statements is refutable. Getting better implies you have been worse—a premise inconsistent with a Divine Identity. "It's all good" is mistaken for truth, but the truth is that Divine Nature (GOD) is Good. The Nature of Good is the spiritual ideal, without an opposing nature of evil. Your True Nature is

Good, and you bring forth good from your experience because I AM Good. The experience itself is not necessarily good.

"Things have a way of turning out all right" is a soothing, hopeful thought, but it does not reflect the truth that things—internal as well as external conditions—are powerless in and of themselves. The truth is things are acted upon by consciousness. By turning to our correct consciousness, Divine Consciousness, we perceive and shape things.

Affirmation is not possibility thinking, either. Possibility thinking says there's a chance for an optimal outcome. Possibility thinking is chance thinking, throwing the dice in hopes the odds are in our favor. Possibility thinking is reflected in these words spoken by someone job searching: "I know there is a better-fitting position for me. The employer I am seeking is now seeking me." Entirely possible, and certainly a helpful thought, but not a statement of truth. The truth is: *Divine Nature (GOD) is Infinite Wisdom. I AM Divine Wisdom discerning how and where to offer my greatest gifts and talents.*

Affirmation is not wishful thinking. Wishful thinking is magical thinking, or dreaming of better circumstances and declaring them as fact. Saying to myself "I am a millionaire" does not make me a millionaire. Declaring "My lungs breathe easily" does not instantaneously cure chest congestion. We do not wield affirmations like the fairy dust that turned Cinderella into a princess. The truth is *Divine Nature (GOD) is inexhaustible abundance. I AM Divine Abundance. By the power of Divine Abundance, I live richly. Divine Nature (GOD) is free-flowing, ever-renewing vitality. I AM Divine Vitality. By the power of Divine Vitality, I bless my every breath.*

Attributes of Effective Affirmations

Positive thinking, possibility thinking, and wishful thinking all may serve a purpose in cultivating an optimistic, hopeful attitude. An optimistic, hopeful attitude can expand our awareness and point to the truth. Affirmations are more than optimistic and hopeful thoughts; they are statements of truth stemming from spiritual realization—they are realization thinking. Realization thinking is an inner conviction of truth that is independent of outer circumstances. Affirmations, therefore, are declarations about Divine Nature and our Divine Identity and usually arise from study, prayer, and meditation. As such, affirmations are recognizable by particular attributes: Affirmations focus on the present. They emphasize *being* rather than *doing*. And they center on unalterable truth.

Focus on the present: Statements predicting a future outcome are not affirmations. Affirmations address a here-and-now Divine Reality. For example, instead of saying "I am attracting the ideal life partner," you might say, "**I AM** Divine Love, attractive and inviting Divine Love." With this shift in awareness, you realize that attracting a partner is not your mission. You are Divine Love, and Divine Love is yours.

Emphasize *being* rather than *doing*: Saying "I maintain my ideal weight" or "I love and accept myself" addresses your human action. Instead, affirm your spiritual nature. "*I AM* Divine Order, balanced and stabilized. I AM embracing, nurturing Divine Love." Doing arises from being. Affirmations prompt actions consistent with truth. Knowing you are Divine Order, or Divine Love, changes your mission, so to speak, from fixing something about yourself to living these Divine Capacities.

Center on unalterable truth: effective affirmations direct your attention away from changing conditions and toward unchangeable truth. Saying "I always have enough money" is not necessarily a true statement. Chances are, sometimes you have enough money and sometimes you do not. Instead, tell yourself the enduring truth: "I AM Divine Abundance, an ever-flowing stream of plenty." Why is this effective? Because you see that your richness is invulnerable to variations in your bank account. With truth in mind, now you are available for and may easily attract yourself into rich experiences and magnificent possibilities independent of your personal means.

How to Practice Affirmation in Prayer

At any time and in any situation, we can form affirmations. One day, feeling hurried while driving in my car, I was jolted into realizing how closely I was trailing the driver ahead of me when she slammed on her brakes—I just missed colliding with her vehicle. In my freshly awakened state, I affirmed, *I AM harmonious Divine Love on the road.* Don't you wish more drivers affirmed *I AM harmonious Divine Love on the road?*

Just as a piano player in a bar can play a tune on request, our capacity to create effective affirmations on the spot is determined by our practice. We practice affirmation in prayer because in prayer we open ourselves to Divine Nature and the reality of our Divine Identity. In prayer, we penetrate the boundaries of time-space limitations. We free ourselves from "only human" perception. We sense our True Nature. We see through spiritual eyes the truth that had earlier eluded us. We dwell in realization thinking. Words of affirmation arising from realization thinking are, therefore, revelatory. They bring to light our essential nature, which is divine.

In prayer, then, lies our greatest possibility of grasping the magnificent truth underlying our pursuits, responses, and inspired actions. The following recommendations may support you as you practice affirmation in prayer.

Be Specific

Construct affirmations using particular words that clearly describe the truth arising in your awareness. This can be challenging because experiencing truth is different from stating truth, and truth is generally experienced in a transcendent, wordless state. Reaching for words that authenticate the spiritual experience, we often apply language that is vague and impotent. For example: "I claim my rightful consciousness." "I am one with the One."

Translate spiritual experience into language by contemplating some of the attributes of Divine Nature and then selecting one that gives you goose bumps. Divine Nature (GOD) is Love, Life, Abundance, Power, Strength, Order, Imagination, Joy, Peace, and so much more. Choose any of the divine characteristics you relate to, or a synonym, such as Harmony (for Love) or Steadfastness (for Strength). Meditate upon the meaning of the words and the actions that might spring from them. Now, identify with that Divine Attribute! Name yourself that! *"I AM Divine Harmony." "I AM Divine Strength standing in the truth."*

Employ Potent Language

Notice the difference in the following two statements. Which of these affirmations makes you want to stand up and cheer?

I AM Divine Good. I accept only the good.

I AM expansive Divine Good, reaching for and grabbing the sweetness of life.

An effective affirmation captivates our attention and moves us from doubt to faith and from fear to reassurance. Therefore, reach for the most compelling language—juicy words that stir your imagination and seem irresistible. Feelings must be engaged. Head and heart must be united; otherwise, you work against yourself. If your intellect crafts wonderful words, but your heart does not believe them, your affirmation frustrates rather than supports. You experience inner conflict rather than inspiration.

A prominent affirmation in Unity circles was written by Unity's cofounder Charles Fillmore in the final year of his long life: "I fairly sizzle with zeal and enthusiasm and spring forth with a mighty faith to do the things that ought to be done by me." (*Atom-Smashing Power of Mind* [Unity Books: Unity Village MO, 1949], 13).

Fillmore could have said, "I AM Divine Energy doing what I need to do, with faith." He probably would not have become famous for that statement, at any age.

Reach for Comprehension of the Most Accessible, Unarguable Truth

When I do not feel well in my body, repeating a statement that appears unbelievable to me does not help me. Repeating "I am whole and well" when I do not feel well becomes wishful thinking rather than a truth I can claim. You might argue that "I am whole and well" is *absolute* truth and therefore the ultimate affirmation. Certainly "I am whole and well" is absolute truth. However, when my body is shivering in a fever or aching in pain, can I claim I am whole and well? I cannot. I find it helpful, therefore, to latch on to an accessible, unarguable truth. I might say:

- GOD *is ever-renewing Divine Life; therefore, I AM ever-renewing Divine Life.*

- *Every cell of my body is pulsing Divine Life.*

- *All that* GOD *is is my True Nature. All-encompassing Wholeness is my True Nature.*

- *I AM Divine. All-inclusive Wholeness and exhilarating wellness are natural to me.*

- *I rest and relax in my True State of Being, well-being.*

Notice that none of the above statements predict an outcome or reflect wishful thinking. Each states the truth emphatically, clearly, in language that connects feeling and thought. Effective affirmations such as these lead to your expressing the truth you comprehend.

Truth never changes—our understanding of truth changes. The affirmation we state tomorrow may well be closer to absolute truth than the words we can claim today. Perhaps tomorrow we can say, with conviction, "I AM whole and well." However, words of truth that resonate today—not *maybe tomorrow*—promote truer living today.

Repeat Affirmations Often

When you repeat effective affirmations, you train your consciousness. The more you impress upon your mind and heart words of truth, the more truth becomes a living reality in your experience. This is why many teachers of affirmation recommend their students offer a set number of repetitions daily or plaster mirrors and dashboards with written affirmations. Such reminders can act like flashing red lights ahead of us on the highway. They grab our attention and shake us into alertness.

The practice of repeating affirmations is helpful, as long as you do not resort to superstitious practice. Superstitious practice stems from the belief that if you recite this particular affirmation x number of times for x number of days, your dreams will all come true. This is not spiritual practice. It is treating affirmations as good-luck charms.

Along the same lines, Jesus of Nazareth advised against "vain repetition" because pointlessly repeating phrases you've simply read or heard will not cause those words to take hold in consciousness. Vain repetition is void of feelings. Feelings are essential to affirmations, because truth does not take hold solely in the intellect. Truth is felt! Every repetition ought to be conscious, renewing your comprehension and conviction of the truth. Truth needs to be understood and felt, for then it becomes your dominant reality.

Practice Affirmations Alone and Following Denials

As part of a daily prayer plan (addressed in chapter 5), affirmations cultivate a spiritualized consciousness. Practiced in prayer, affirmations repeatedly remind you of the truth of your Divine

Identity, fortifying you so that you might live more fully into your Divine Identity. Realized and felt affirmations, written or recited, in original language or lifted from literature, form a foundation for dedicated spiritual practice.

When practicing affirmations unattached to denials, pay attention to your *felt* response as you repeat each statement. Become sensitized to niggling doubt and cynicism. For example, if during a long recovery from illness you repeat, "I AM radiant Divine Life upholding my body's health and vitality," notice whether you sense subtle disbelief, perhaps a whispering thought of *I don't feel healthy*. Whenever you sense a thought or feeling contrary to spiritual truth, go back to practicing denials before your affirmations.

Study, Pray, and Meditate Regularly

Realization thinking arises from a spiritualized consciousness. Spiritual study, prayer, and meditation cultivate spiritualized consciousness. Affirmations contain a spiritual vernacular. When practiced and repeated often, affirmations become part of our everyday manner of speaking. In our process of conditioning ourselves to identify with Divine Nature (GOD), Divine Nature becomes natural to us. During those times when we slink back toward an "only human" sense of ourselves, we have access to familiar language that acts like a tap on the shoulder calling us to attention.

By all means, therefore, practice the tool of affirmation. Over time, you may find that affirmations enter your awareness, fully formed, without conscious effort. These are affirmations arising from realization thinking. Often they contain reassurance during times of spiritual doubt or fear. Several years ago, for example, when I had been released from my position at Unity of Omaha, I felt acute fear about my calling as a minister, for which I was in the middle of studying; my financial well-being; and my family's capacity to manage through a time of significant transition. A few nights into this transition, I awoke suddenly out of deep sleep, sat up in bed, and heard in my mind *Watch, Linda. Something wonderful is happening for you.*

I took my wake-up call as a truth in which to stand throughout the following months. Every day I looked for and found "something wonderful." I felt convinced I AM wonderful Divine Life happening. To the amazement of my colleagues, within three months I had an offer from Unity in San Antonio, even though I had not yet completed ministerial training.

Live the Truth Revealed in Affirmation

Become a living affirmation through conscious, authentic action springing from words of affirmation. But do not limit affirmation to words alone. Words alone would be like describing a sumptuous feast but not partaking of it. Following words of affirmation, exercise your Divine Power of Imagination by envisioning what living the truth might look like. Following I AM Divine Audacity, you might envision yourself approaching your boss for a past-due conversation about the promotion you had been promised a year ago. You might imagine taking the microphone at your parent's birthday celebration and showering your parent with words of praise and blessing.

Then, of course, do it. You are, after all, Divine Audacity.

Pattern for Practice of Denials and Affirmations

The following three scenarios provide a pattern for practicing denials and affirmations. Incorporate them into your prayer time using a journal or in conversation with a supportive prayer partner.

Example 1: The Truth of Plenty

I am praying for my house to sell.

Facts:

- The house has been on the market for months with no buyer in sight.
- I have purchased a new house.
- With two house payments, I have been depleting my savings.

Feelings:

- Worry—I am running out of money and soon could be homeless.
- Insecurity—The rug could be pulled out from under me; my life could collapse.
- Disillusionment—The Law of Attraction is not working. I intended this move to happen swiftly and easily. Either I am not doing something right, or the law is bogus.

Underlying Beliefs:

- There is not enough to go around: not enough money for me and not enough people wanting a new home.
- I can be harmed by unforeseen circumstances.
- I cannot trust my inspired desires.
- Life is unreliable. I cannot count on things going my way.

Denial (Release/Elimination):

I set aside any concern about my well-being right now, refusing any resting place in my awareness for worry and fear. I shush compulsive worry about money and possessions. I deny not-enoughness in my consciousness. I refuse to indulge in another moment of apprehension about this situation. I withdraw my attention from these circumstances, refusing them power over my life.

Furthermore, I turn my thoughts away from distrust in what could happen. I stop hysterical imaginings and refuse to indulge concern that I could be harmed. I deny any room in my mind or heart for fearful thoughts of unworthiness. I withdraw my attention from fleeting fears for my future. I do not squander another moment thinking that something is going wrong.

Affirmation:

In a universe overflowing with enough for everyone, I affirm I have all I need in every way. I claim the Divine Ideas that I use to manifest my good. Evidence of good is all around me, in the blessing of my new home, in my relationships, and in the fact that I am sheltered, clothed, and nourished. I relax in appreciation of all the wonderful possibilities before me.

Knowing Divine Life is always moving forward, onward, and upward, I ride on the current of Divine Life now, today, rather than waiting for some acceptable outcome down the road. I trust in GOD/Good for there is only GOD/Good in my Divine Life.

Living Affirmation:

- I use my faculty of Divine Imagination to see the next owner of this house settled in: smiling while looking out at the scenery through the picture window, cozying up to a loved one on a sofa in the family room, soaking in the whirlpool bathtub (maybe I don't want to imagine what *that* looks like!).

- I go through each room in ritual or in my mind, blessing the space for the next owner.

- I look intently for evidence of my abundance and prosperity. I appreciate meaningful work and sustaining income. I look for evidence of where else I have used Divine Ideas and my innate prosperity to experience my good.

- I notice ways I am treated to discounts or no-charge for goods and services. I marvel at people's generosity toward me. I bless every bill coming in and every payment going out.

- I feel grateful for everything I have. I bless all that flows from me and to me.

Example 2: Secure in Truth

I am praying about trouble with my ex-spouse.

Facts:

- The ex-spouse has initiated relentless and cruel legal challenges over custody of the children.
- I never know when the next false charge is coming.

Feelings:

- Threatened—One of these times my ex-spouse could convince the court and take my children away from me.
- Dread—I could become penniless because of exorbitant legal expenses.
- Helplessness—This is impossible. I cannot do anything to improve this situation.

Underlying Beliefs:

- I have absolutely no control over my life or my children's lives.
- My ex-spouse is spiritually unreachable, wholly opposed to GOD, evil.
- Malevolent forces could take away everyone and everything I cherish.
- Life is frightening.

Denial (Release/Elimination):
My ex-spouse cannot possibly threaten my well-being, because no person or power exists outside of GOD. I reject the idea that anything or anyone external to me could have power over me. I release the power I have given to evil and reject it outright as untruth. I renounce any thought of negativity about my ex-spouse and about my circumstances. I deny the power of my mistaken thoughts and beliefs.

In addition, I refuse to devote another moment to dreadful imaginings. I no longer identify myself as a fearful "only human."

Affirmation:
There is only One Power, GOD/Good. I AM Divine Power expressing in every thought, word, and action. Divine Power brings all things to light and blesses all that is good. Good is happening within me and all around me, and I have divine eyes to see it.

I proceed in this situation as a Divine Force for Good. Divine Strength is my capacity to hold to the truth even in adverse circumstances. Divine Love is my capacity to respond in harmony with and from the truth I know. I breathe deeply in each moment, steady in my Divine Identity.

Living Affirmation:

- I imagine my children loved and cared for. I envision them gloriously happy, industrious, and self-knowing. Every day, I bless them in my thoughts and feelings about their well-being.

- I look for and find reasons to be appreciative. I appreciate my legal counsel, capably supporting my children and me. I appreciate every moment in my children's company.

- I deliberately transform my thoughts about my ex-spouse. Even when I do not recognize it, I know the truth of my ex-spouse's Divine Identity.

- I respond to every summons and every correspondence from a consciousness of clarity. I turn these circumstances into opportunities for truth to triumph.

Example 3: It's About Time

I am praying about whether or not to embark on a new project.

Facts:

- The project I am considering appeals to me on many levels. It would use many of my strengths and skills, contribute to a worthy cause, and further my career.

- My calendar is full.

- I have a history of taking on more than I can manage well.

Feelings:

- Fascination—I feel thrilled about the possibilities.

- Hesitation—I feel concerned about whether I could see this through. If something more urgent came up, would I have to relinquish this project? Or perhaps I will get bored with it and not give it all the attention it requires. What am I thinking? I don't have the time for this!

Underlying Beliefs:

- There is never enough time.
- I cannot trust my inner guidance.
- I am never satisfied.

Denial (Release/ Elimination):
I relinquish attention on stress and worry about my use of time. I reject the thoughts that time could run out, that important things could be left undone, and that I could lose in any way. I stop giving power to the clock. I refuse to be run by the clock.

I deny the power I have given to my false beliefs about time. Also, I stop distrusting my own inner knowing. I give up vacillating between eagerness and hesitation. I renounce the idea that I could never do enough to feel fulfilled.

Affirmation:
Wonderful opportunities catch my attention because I AM Divine Imagination capable of vividly picturing the possibilities. Life is juicy, rich, and infinitely interesting to me! My Divine Life is limitless, and I am free to explore any and every prospect.

I AM Divine Wisdom. Every moment I consciously select where to place my attention and to what to devote my time. Time stands still for me as I wholeheartedly savor the moment.

Living Affirmation:

- By the power of my Divine Imagination, I create my fulfilling life. I live each day successfully, joyously, and appreciatively.

- I contemplate the possibilities of weaving this project into my schedule. By the power of my Divine Wisdom, I become clear so that my yes or my no is emphatic, arising from enduring truth rather than fluctuating emotion.

Now that you have a pattern for practicing denials and affirmations, these tools can be incorporated into daily prayer practice. Practicing denials and affirmations daily is a sure way to remember truth when truth is most needed.

Talk to Yourself

- How do you recognize a need for denials? What happens in your body, mind, and emotions when you are, shall I say, full of it?

- You know that you have been successful in the practice of denial when your thoughts, words, and actions no longer fixate on the false beliefs you had unconsciously harbored. Share with others a success story in your practice of denial.

- Reflect upon how you practiced affirmation in the past. How much of your practice involved wishful thinking, trying to convince yourself what you said was true, or repeating affirmations as you would rub a rabbit's foot?

- Select an issue in your life right now about which to practice denial and affirmation in prayer. Follow the format suggested in the examples just prior to this section.

Chapter 5

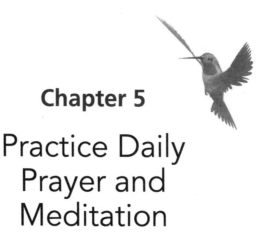

Practice Daily Prayer and Meditation

Watch carefully, and you will find that there are some things, even in the active unselfish doing, which would better be left undone than that you should neglect regular meditation.
—*Harriette Emilie Cady,* Lessons in Truth: A Course of Twelve Lessons in Practical Christianity *(1919)*

Daily prayer and meditation practice builds spiritual consciousness.

A 2008 Brandeis University poll suggested 90 percent of people pray daily. People of all faiths follow religiously prescribed practices that include reading scripture, reciting memorized prayers, saying grace before meals, and other directives to turn our minds toward the divine. My guess is that a majority of this 90 percent prays quickly and momentarily, rather than devoting a segment of time each day to prayer and meditation.

Daily practice of prayer and meditation leads to heightened spiritual realization. Spiritual realization supports living in spiritually conscious ways—in the world but not of it. Daily prayer practice builds spiritual muscle in much the same way physical exercise builds muscles in the body. Unity cofounder Myrtle Fillmore urged people to pray daily, promising in her book *How to Let God Help You* "Your mind will become keen, awake, alert, and illumined, and your body temple will be filled with new life. You will be inspired with practical ideas that will enable you to succeed in a larger way."

Once our eyes open after a night's rest, most people begin a cycle of thinking and doing for the next sixteen hours or longer, nonstop. Our culture supports a frenetic, always-on connectivity with the world around us. Moments perfect for pausing—sitting in a waiting room, for example—that in past generations would have been considered a respite are today crammed with texting, checking email, and keeping abreast of up-to-the-minute news. Our brains are laden with information and exhausted by overuse. Practicing daily prayer may seem like one more duty easier skipped for an extra half hour of needed sleep.

Overcome Obstacles to Daily Prayer Practice

In prayer classes I teach, many students admit to struggling over daily prayer. They sincerely desire to reap the rewards of daily prayer, evidenced by their participation in a prayer class. They seem to be in search of a singular technique or a compelling motivation to make daily prayer habitual.

Among the reasons people seem to struggle over daily prayer are these three: we believe we cannot possibly dedicate the necessary time, we cannot seem to sit still, and we experience no benefit from daily prayer. Let's examine these discouraging mindsets by emphasizing strategies to overcome them.

Time Constraints

I have no time. I am overscheduled from morning till night. I sleep too little as it is. I hardly have time to brush my teeth in the morning. My children wake me, and from that point on, I am on duty. My work schedule varies from day to day. I have no down time or time alone, ever.

Time waits for no one. You can't see time or hold it in your hand. You can spend time and invest time but not own time. You can kill time but not create time. The time you save today cannot be banked for tomorrow. Time is a mental construct: insubstantial, though it feels concrete; elusive as well as noticeable; boundless even as you count it down. Ten minutes can feel like ten hours, as when waiting for a loved one's doctor to confirm that surgery was successful. Conversely, a full day can pass in the seeming blink of an eye, as when reuniting with a beloved friend.

On the surface, a simple remedy for the problem of time might be to schedule time, the one control we can exert over time, to prioritize prayer. For many people, though, wrestling with time is a long-standing habit having nothing at all to do with time. If the struggle is an ontological one, it becomes a question of purpose, meaning, and self-definition. Those of us who feel constrained by time, hurried, or pressed for time usually also have internalized messages about our worth in relation to our accomplishments. We have come to believe that if we *do* enough, we will *be* enough.

If this is your issue, work it out in prayer. Practice denials and affirmations pertinent to the meaning you have attached to time. For example:

> *I deny the power I have given time to limit what is possible for me to accomplish. I affirm I AM limitless Divine Order suspending time as I wholeheartedly do all that is mine to do.*

> *I deny the false belief that my worth is measured by my achievements. I affirm All That Is is my True Nature. By my very being, I am a blessing.*

If prayer is important to you, you will work it into your busy day. I know someone who began a daily prayer practice years ago while enrolled in my prayer class. Having established the habit, he kept his appointment even when his commute lengthened to one-and-a-half hours one way and his workday stretched from dawn to dusk. He kept up his daily prayer practice because he derived great benefit from doing so. He reported that despite increasing work demand, he remained more centered, positive, and fulfilled because of daily prayer.

Work out the problem of time as creatively as possible. A mother I know created a prayer opportunity in the quiet time after lunch each day. She could have occupied that hour with any number of other activities; she chose prayer because the cumulative effects of daily prayer supported her intention to be a good mother. When her children no longer needed daily naps, they read or played alone in their rooms during quiet time, while their mom continued to dedicate that time to prayer.

The words you use to characterize your use of time can have unconscious consequences. Simply selecting different language can shift your awareness and therefore your attitude about prayer time. The phrase *spending time* can have the connotation of depleting or even wasting time. Instead, change to the phrase *investing time*, which promotes an attitude of accumulating value. Likewise, instead of thinking of prayer as discipline, consider it devotion.

Restlessness

I can't sit still, even for a few moments. My mind wanders. I feel restless. I cannot gain control over my thoughts. I can hardly wait for the timer to go off. I feel fidgety and uncomfortable. Every little sound catches my attention. I get nowhere. It seems pointless.

Periods of restlessness during prayer are common. When restlessness periodically prevents you from enjoying prayer practice, your remedy could be as simple as eliminating caffeine from your diet or increasing the amount of time you give to the first phase of prayer, relaxation (addressed later in this chapter). When occurring repeatedly even after such modifications, though, restless periods usually point to a deeper issue, the issue of avoidance.

We avoid prayer when we do not want to see ourselves clearly, when we feel afraid of going deep, when we sense an inner calling requiring commitment and discipline. Restlessness may be your way of screaming *I don't want to be the Light of the World!* Don't believe it. It's not true. We only resist what we most desire when we feel incapable of living up to the spiritual demand of our high calling. Persistence in prayer is our best chance to become equipped for being the Light of the World.

Frankly, I find it challenging to outwit restlessness. That is why I rely on prayer partners, inspiring texts, and an occasional prerecorded guided visualization. Sometimes the truth expressed by others reaches out to me like a lifeline, steadying me and drawing me back to centeredness.

You also might avoid prayer because in prayer "nothing is hidden that will not be disclosed, nor is anything secret that will not become known and come to light" (Luke 8:17). You may feel afraid that your self-perceived character flaws and unloving behaviors will be exposed in prayer and that you will feel worse, not better, about yourself. Nothing could be further from the truth. Jesus of Nazareth's declaration, echoed in the Gospels of Matthew and Thomas, assures us that the greatest secret of all, our True Nature, will be revealed. At times when the great truth of your Divine Identity seems obscured from your view, persistence in prayer will reveal it.

Misguided Expectation

Nothing happens—nothing during prayer and nothing afterward. Prayer doesn't work. It doesn't make any difference. Why bother? I must not be doing it right. I don't hear voices or see images, and I don't get answers. I don't find GOD in my prayer time. Something amazing should happen when I pray. I should feel the spirit. All I hear are my own thoughts. I am not inspired.

In my sixth month of residence at Kripalu ashram in 1976, I was longing for the phenomena many of my brothers and sisters appeared to have during times of community meditation. All around me, bodies stretched into ecstatic postures, faces glowed, and voices emitted otherworldly sounds. I felt sure I was missing out and convinced I was spiritually deficient. One morning, our guru surprisingly redirected our attention away from these kinds of "phenomena" during meditation. While I cannot quote his exact words, our guru said, essentially:

When, over time, we consciously live from realization of our Divine Identity, more often than not our purpose for praying is being achieved.

> You are enjoying blissful sensations while you sit here, but the benefit of meditation is a growing spiritual consciousness, not phenomenon. From now on, there will be no external phenomena during group meditation—no calling out or spontaneous movements. You will return to the basics so that your practice will benefit your daily living.

Our rightful expectation is not for a swift answer to our pressing question, James Earl Jones's voice resolving our indecisiveness, or even momentary bliss. When, over time, we consciously live from realization of our Divine Identity, more often than not our purpose for praying is being achieved.

Recommended Format for Daily Prayer

Relax so you can concentrate; concentrate so you can meditate; meditate so you can realize; realize so you can appreciate; appreciate so you can relax.

Relaxation

At first, the idea of including relaxation as a phase of prayer might appear unreasonable. Relaxation seems counter to what you may have learned in religious education, when you were told to sit up, place folded hands on your lap, and pay attention, or when Buddhist monks would smack you on the back if you slumped over during arduous hours of mindfulness meditation. Relaxation, however, is a crucial beginning to successful daily prayer.

Relaxation is important because physical discomfort and mental disturbance prevent our realization of Divine Unity/Oneness, which becomes fulfilled through prayer. The relaxation phase of prayer slows body processes, eases physical discomfort, and quiets extraneous thinking. Beginning a time of prayer without first assuring relaxation would be like exercising cold muscles or embarking on a long-distance drive with an empty gas tank—frustrating, irritating, and unsuccessful. The following are some suggestions for practicing physical and mental relaxation at the start of prayer:

> **Prepare the environment.** If possible, designate a prayer chair in a serene setting for daily prayer. Light a candle and display sacred objects, if you desire. When you cannot designate a particular space for prayer, do what is possible to diminish distractions and achieve relaxation.

In a home bustling with the activity of little children, for example, enlist the support of other adults so you can carve out a space and time for prayer every day. Keep in mind that the environment for prayer and meditation need not be elaborate or pristine. Simple, tidy, and comfortable will do.

Relax your body. Whether accompanied by inspiring music or silence, open your chest and flex your spine with sweeping arm gestures. Or, move slowly through the classic yoga posture surya namaskara, the sun salutation. Follow your body's natural prompting to stretch and relax before sitting in prayer.

Breathe consciously. Many people breathe shallowly and, when told to breathe deeply, breathe in through the mouth into the upper chest. Yoga practitioners know how to draw in rich, deep breaths that maximize oxygen absorption in the body and, as important, send relaxation messages to the brain. Study and practice yoga breathing exercises to focus awareness on the present moment and clear mental tension. Combine breathing and relaxing body movement to heighten relaxation.

Clear mental tension. When something is on your mind, when feeling concern or questioning, replaying a troublesome conversation, or holding an unwanted thought, you crave the relaxation of mental tension to pave the way for an enriching prayer session. It is not necessary to have solved a problem or reconciled an issue before prayer—because, of course, the activity of prayer itself can lead to resolution. It is important to reduce mental agitation, however. Sometimes breathing and stretching alone suffice. At other times, downloading all your concerns onto paper relieves mental overload. In addition, using the tools of denial and affirmation clears contrary thinking and anchors truth.

Relaxation practices enjoin body and mind in a comfortable and conscious state of being. Restful, yet awake; relaxed, yet attentive. The time invested in the relaxation phase of prayer paves the way to spiritual realization.

Concentration

In keeping with spiritual law—also called the Law of Mind Action, or the Law of Attraction—what you focus upon in consciousness expands in consciousness. Therefore, once relaxation is achieved at the start of prayer, you turn your thoughts toward truth and gently focus your attention on a captivating truth idea. How do you select a truth idea to focus upon? Sometimes an affirmation you have read occupies your thinking. Truth spoken by a prayer partner, or heard on a recorded message, may kindle your desire for deeper realization. At other times, you may construct an affirmation based upon your perceived need for it. If you employed the tools of denial and affirmation beforehand, you may benefit from concentrating on that affirmation in this phase of prayer.

Concentration is a vital phase of prayer practice in which you magnify a truth idea by holding it uppermost in mind. Concentration builds up and strengthens spiritual consciousness by magnetizing similar thoughts and multiplying the effects of truth, leading to spiritual illumination. When concentrating on the statement *I AM Divine Abundance*, for example, you notice other thoughts arising, such as *With every breath I demonstrate Divine Abundance. I live and give abundantly. I AM a rich blessing, richly blessed.* Concentrating on Divine Abundance, we become aware of where abundance is flowing in our lives—abundance of health, loving relationships, meaningful work, and money.

Concentrate on *I AM* affirmations that bring you into alignment with Divine Nature and your Divine Identity:

- *I AM expansive Divine Life, Love, and Wisdom.*
- *I AM the unifying power of Divine Love.*
- *I AM a rippling stream of Divine Peace.*

To practice concentration in prayer, repeat the selected *I AM* affirmation as you would a mantra (sacred syllables repeated in Eastern spiritual practices), returning to the repetition whenever you notice your thoughts have wandered. As you repeat your *I AM* affirmation, invite spiritual understanding until you are no longer consciously aware of thinking, until you are entering meditation.

Now, after relaxation and concentration, you are about to arrive at the heart of prayer—meditation. Unfortunately, most people, much of the time, stop here. We feel a little better than when we began, a little more centered. We gave our twenty minutes to the effort. We return to the activity of the day, unaware we were on the threshold of breakthrough awareness—piercing physical consciousness to discover within an expansive spiritual reality.

Meditation can be a stand-alone practice for purposes of quieting the mind and stilling the body. Meditation within prayer practice, however, prepares you for what is to come—realization of your Divine Identity and, therefore, your capacity to respond to life circumstances accordingly. In prayer, concentration is not the final step.

Make time for meditation.

Meditation

Meditation instruction and practice varies from one faith tradition to another. In Buddhist mindfulness meditation, students are instructed to maintain a relaxed awareness of the present moment, which may include physical sensations, passing thoughts, and interruptions. Centering prayer is a Christian practice of devoted attention on a name or a quality of GOD, similar to Hindu meditation upon mantra. Each of these disciplines, labeled *meditation*, relates more exactly to the *concentration* phase of prayer. Practitioners of these disciplines may or may not proceed to the state of nonawareness named, for our purposes, the *meditation* phase of prayer.

Although no thing happens in meditation, meditation leads to the greatest thing—spiritual realization.

Meditation as a phase of prayer centers you in the heart of your heart, your Divine Identity, in a deep and restful silence. Here, in a nontime/nonspace reality, your personal sense of self recedes. This reality is indescribable. No language can effectively explain it.

Although no thing happens in meditation, meditation leads to the greatest thing—spiritual realization.

Resting in the silence occurs not by exerting effort but by withdrawing effort.

Considering we function mostly by effort, the nondoing of meditation confuses us. Although we are used to being rewarded for effort, in meditation, effort only frustrates, by delaying our experience of the silence. The silence is a delicate state. The second we think we are experiencing the silence, we are not, because thinking is a state of awareness. This is true about experience in general—the moment we exclaim, "How beautiful is the sunset!" we are out of the experience and thinking about the experience that has passed.

The challenges most of us encounter in meditation practice are many. Extraneous thoughts intrude. External sights and sounds distract. We fall asleep. We come to only question whether we "did it" or not. We slip into and fall out of the moment many times over. We watch the clock. We later recognize we may have actually been in the silence for seconds at a time. Considering the delicacy of the meditation state, seconds in the silence is generally considered successful meditation practice.

My friend Rudi enjoys tea made from jasmine "pearls," tender jasmine leaves compressed into miniscule balls. A perfect cup of jasmine tea is made, Rudi says, by boiling water and then removing it from the heat source for exactly one minute, during which the temperature will drop from 212 degrees to 180 degrees Fahrenheit. The hot water is poured into a cup containing five or six pearls so that, minutes later, the jasmine pearls will have opened and infused the water with their delightful taste and fragrance.

For a perfect cup of jasmine tea, all the elements must work together precisely. Imagine, therefore, the perfectly aligned body/mind/spirit state of oneness in the silence. Imagine how, in a split second, an ankle itch can disturb the body, the washing machine signal can distract the mind, and an *ah-ha* or *uh-oh* can intrude on the silence. A slight shift in alignment can break the state of non-awareness. This would be all right, if we did not attach negative meaning to it. We tell ourselves we have failed in our attempts to meditate. No, we have not failed. We have practiced.

Meditation is the most elusive phase of prayer; it is also the most compelling. Those who persist in practice eventually regard meditation not as a scheduled discipline but as a refreshing necessity, like air and water. Rosemary Fillmore Rhea told this story about her grandfather, Unity cofounder Charles Fillmore:

> I learned about prayer from my grandfather . . . He was different from other grandfathers; when he was not involved in conversation or activities he went into "the Silence" [meditated]. It was so much a part of him that I assumed all grandfathers meditated. However, one Saturday some school friends came to play and they noticed my grandfather sitting with his eyes closed, but not sleeping. When we went outside, they asked me why my grandfather just sat with his eyes closed. I replied, "He is in the Silence, of course. Doesn't your grandfather sit in the Silence?" They assured me that their grandfathers didn't and wondered about the Silence. I explained he was praying.

Elusive though meditation may seem to be, resting in the silence is our highest intention in prayer, because out of the silence comes our deepest realization.

Realization

Spiritual realization is the fruit of prayer. As a phase of prayer, realization follows relaxation, concentration, and meditation because these earlier phases prepare you, focus your attention, and center you in truth. Realization occurs when truth becomes real to you, no longer theoretical. You get it! Whereas before you believed it, now you know it. It doesn't matter whether anyone else knows it or whether you have seen its manifestation. You now live into this truth. Realized truth becomes lived truth.

Realized truth becomes lived truth.

A truth idea you had intellectually understood to be true now reveals its expansive meaning and implications and how you can use it in daily living.

In daily prayer focused on Divine Life, Myrtle Fillmore demonstrated realization and described her thought process about it in this excerpt from her journal:

> Life has to be guided by intelligence in making all forms. The same law works in my own body. Life is simply a form of energy and has to be guided and directed in man's body by his intelligence. How do we communicate intelligence? By thinking and talking, of course. Then it

flashed upon me that I might talk to the life in every part of my body and have it do just what I wanted.

Fillmore's realization thinking led her to direct Divine Life into her body until her body displayed its natural wholeness. Instead of dying of the tuberculosis she contracted in her forties, she lived until the age of eighty-seven.

To practice realization in prayer, linger after meditation. Ponder the meaning of your *I AM* affirmation from earlier in your prayer session. Record your realization thinking in your journal.

Realization is not limited to a specified period of time in prayer. Nor does realization necessarily become obvious during this phase of prayer. Whether or not you gain a conscious, clear thought of realization during prayer, observe your thoughts, words, and actions over time. You may discover interesting changes and patterns that you may not have realized in those moments or even immediately following them. Spiritual realization becomes lived truth.

Appreciation

Ending a prayer session in a state of appreciation is natural as well as beneficial. Sometimes this phase of prayer is named *thanksgiving* or *gratitude*. I prefer *appreciation*, because of its shades of meaning. To appreciate a thing is to regard it as valuable, to turn your attention toward it, and to increase its value by your recognition. All of these aspects of appreciation apply in the final phase of daily prayer.

We too often express appreciation lazily. We say, "Thank you, God," even when we know god is not a person. I have listened spellbound while colleagues employ luscious vocabulary in words of prayer, only to feel dispirited when they close with a perfunctory "Thank you, God."

Experiment with words of appreciation not directed at a person, such as *How blessed I feel to know that I AM wise. Everything in my world appears right and in its place now that I see through eyes of Divine Order. I appreciate my growing realization of my Divine Identity.* Instead of "Thank you, God, for the rain," you can employ evocative language of appreciation, such as *I feel singing-in-the-rain, puddle-jumping, mud-pie-making, happy about the rain!* Instead of "Thank you, God, for your peace," try *Divine Peace now emanates from me in ever-expanding ripples, steeping everything and everyone in tranquility.*

Appreciation is not limited to words. Practice expressing appreciation wordlessly. Savor the moment of closing prayer and returning awareness to your external environment. Intend to look upon your space, and your life, appreciatively. Tell yourself about the value of your prayer practice, your room, your family, and your work. The magnificent effect of appreciation is that it fulfills itself—appreciation appreciates! Daily prayer practice provides a foundation of spiritual realization out of which you can live confidently.

Talk to Yourself

- If you are not in the habit of daily prayer, reflect upon what may be in the way of your making it so. Cough up all your excuses, write each one on a scrap of paper, laugh about them, and then tear up the scraps into miniscule pieces. Dig a hole in the ground and let the scraps become fertilizer, because that's all they are worth. Take a deep breath.

- Many people pray a little every day. A little stretching, a little reading, a little asking. What benefits might you gain by investing in deeper aspects of daily prayer such as meditation?

- Considering that meditation is a delicate state of non-awareness, how do you know whether you have been meditating or dozing?

- If you are new to daily prayer practice, commit to it for twenty-one days. A commitment is a promise you make and keep, which means if you lay you head upon your pillow at night without having kept your prayer appointment, you will get out of bed and fulfill your promise before going to sleep.

Chapter 6

Realize Wholeness
Through Prayer

[The] Spirit is happy, whole, free, filled with joy, eternal in Its
existence . . . All your highest hopes and dreams have come
from It. The echo of Its being is in your intellect, the voice of Its
unspoken word is in your mind, the feeling of Its light and life
is in your heart, the emotion of Its imagination is in your soul.

—*Ernest Holmes,* This Thing Called You *(1948)*

**All prayer intentions, whether about material good, relation-
ships, health, or prosperity, have one common aim: realization
of wholeness.**

The number one intention for which most people pray is
healing. We have established that wholeness is natural to
us, because wholeness is an aspect of Divine Nature and
therefore our Divine Identity. When we pray for healing, we actually seek to be reminded of our essential wholeness.

What Is Wholeness?

FreeDictionary.com suggests three definitions of *wholeness*:

1. *Containing all components; complete.* To which I say, all that we know of the Divine Nature—all Life, Love, Wisdom, Strength, Order, and all Divine Capacities—compose our Divine Identity. Whether we are aware of these capacities in any moment, they are innate and only need be recognized, cultivated, and actualized.

2. *Not divided or disjoined; in one unit.* Unity and other New Thought traditions teach that we are individualized expressions of the divine. The word *individual* is commonly defined as "unique," "distinctive," and "particular." But New Thought uses *individual* to mean "indivisible," "inseparable." We cannot be separated out from the source. We are not pieces and parts like what you find in a KFC bucket. Our essential nature is inseparable from Divine Nature.

    The Atharva Veda, a Hindu scripture, supports this definition of wholeness:

    Undivided I am
    Undivided my soul
    Undivided my sight
    Undivided my hearing
    Undivided my inbreathing
    Undivided my outbreathing
    Undivided my diffusive breath
    Undivided the whole of me

3. *Constituting the full amount, extent, or duration.* And we remind ourselves that Divine Nature is not fleeting, partial, or finite. We are fully divine, through and through, eternally.

"Be perfect, therefore, as your heavenly Father is perfect" (Matthew 5:48). These words, credited to Jesus, have been misunderstood, chiefly because of confusion about the meaning of *perfect.* Contemporary connotation of the word *perfect* is "flawless." Study of the original Greek word, however, reveals an entirely different definition. The word *teleios* means "completeness." *Teleios* refers to maturity, as in, being fully grown physically and, more important, spiritually. Jesus was not demanding good behavior. He was calling for remembrance of our essential wholeness, our realization of this truth: life is uninterruptible and incorruptible.

In moments when Jesus called forth wholeness in people who were asking for healing, he said, "You are made whole." Common interpretation of this statement leads us to say that Jesus healed those people. Perhaps, instead, Jesus reminded his listeners of the truth. Chances are Jesus was not saying "You were sick and now I have healed you." Chances are Jesus was saying "You are made from wholeness. You have never been less than whole, because wholeness is your True Nature. You are made whole."

Why Bad Things Happen

If wholeness is our True Nature, why do we get sick? Why do the experiences of others affect us? Why do bad things happen?

When my friend Marjorie was diagnosed with asthma at age forty, the same age her mother contracted asthma, Marjorie worried that she was becoming her mother. It didn't help that when she stared at herself in the mirror, she was disturbed by her growing resemblance to her mother in that regard, as well. My friend believed that she was the cause of her own asthma. Not only had her lifelong disapproval of cigarette smoking led to a "smoker's disease" in her own body but also, more important, her fear of becoming her mother—her worry—had caused it.

My friend's explanation for asthma conforms to common interpretation of the Law of Attraction, popularized by *The Secret* by Rhonda Byrne. The Law of Attraction says that like attracts like. One vibration resonates with the same vibration, as happens when one guitar string is plucked and a nearby guitar string, tuned to the same tone, begins to vibrate as if it too had been plucked. The law *seems* to suggest that thoughts and feelings attract similar circumstances and conditions. Teachers of the Law of Attraction urge their students to monitor their thoughts so that they do not bring unwanted circumstances and conditions into their experience.

Actually, Law of Attraction, also called Law of Mind Action, states that predominant, persistent attitudes and beliefs reproduce after their kind. In other words, we are the creators of our experience. The law does not read that we are the creators of our circumstances, physical conditions, and material belongings—an important distinction.

The Law of Attraction Misunderstood

Do some of the explanations you have heard about why bad things happen seem absurd to you? They do to me. A common interpretation of the Law of Attraction would lead us to believe that a young child displaying signs of autism somehow attracted the condition by hanging around negativity; that, or she made a soul contract before incarnating—another explanation that helps us feel better about unhappy circumstances. It would have us believe that people in our world suffering from hunger and homelessness brought these conditions on themselves. Preposterous!

My discomfort with commonplace interpretations of the Law of Attraction led me to reply to the question *Why did this horrible thing happen?* with a seemingly better, truer question: *How will we respond to this horrible thing?* I discouraged people from asking why, because common answers to the question are distasteful and untrue. We would not for a moment tell a woman who suffered a miscarriage that she attracted this painful occurrence because of some negativity on her part. We would not indict a soldier whose limbs were blown off in war, suggesting he drew this condition to him by the Law of Attraction.

We would not offer explanations such as these because they would crush someone already suffering. Moreover, we really do not believe what we have been preaching.

On September 5, 2001, my younger sister Maureen ended her life by swallowing a mouthful of sleeping pills with whiskey. Serious about her intention, Maureen also covered her head with a plastic bag before she lay down to die. My family and I suffered unspeakable grief. My parents, whose religion is Roman Catholicism, believe that the souls of people who commit suicide cannot enter into heaven. They believe it as a matter of faith. When Maureen died by her own hand, however, the thought of her immortal soul eternally separated from God was so horrifying that they could not accept it. My mother privately told me she was certain a special grace was conferred upon Maureen at the moment of her death, exempting her from an utterly unacceptable fate. When the long-held belief interfered with her greater conviction of Divine Grace and Mercy, my mother laid down a false belief for the truth of wholeness. The truth is, my sister's death by suicide could not corrupt nor interrupt her eternal life that has always been and always shall be whole.

The Highest Expression of the Law of Attraction

We have all experienced a sense of direct connection between our thoughts and feelings and our experiences. In wholeness, we cannot deny body/mind/spirit connectivity, a crosscurrent of messages and impressions eventuating in life experience. We misunderstand the Law of Attraction when we believe we should expect nothing but negative conditions because of our negative thinking. As Dr. Paul Hasselbeck, dean of spiritual education and enrichment at Unity Institute, teaches, we do not attract negative conditions. Rather, we are attracted to negative conditions when we are steeped in a consciousness of negativity. Conditions do not come looking for us. We go looking for them.

Moreover, we limit the Law of Attraction when we recognize its power only in painful, negative conditions. The highest expression of this law is our natural attraction to wholeness! We are attracted to wholeness like the proverbial moth to a flame, because wholeness is our True Nature. All the positive, powerful, perfect moments of our lives confirm our attraction to our innate wholeness. We are attracted to wholeness even when bad things happen. Convinced of our attraction to wholeness, we can radically revise our interpretation of the Law of Attraction when bad things happen. When bad things happen, we can assume that our innate yearning to experience wholeness is the magnet. This is the true answer to the question why.

Once, after the umpteenth time my son and his friends had done some mischief, only Adrian got caught. In his frustration, he cried to me, "How come I'm the only one who always gets caught?"

I replied, "Your True Nature is divine. Everything in you wants to be in integrity with your True Nature."

In my understanding, seemingly negative conditions arise not as punishment for what we've done or not done but because our True Nature reconciles all conditions to itself. Jesus said, "And I, when I am lifted up from the earth, will draw all people to myself" (John 12:32). In metaphysics, people represent thoughts and feelings. Our thoughts and feelings become illumined when we rise above "only human" reactions. Seemingly negative conditions are a kind of practice field for reconciliation.

We could say we have been attracted to seemingly negative conditions by some stinking thinking. Or we could say we have been attracted to them as opportunities to step up into greater awareness of our essential wholeness. The latter reasoning works better for me. I believe it is more compelling and truer than the common explanation. And it works in cases that otherwise do not make sense.

Spiritual Amnesia

It is great, isn't it, to assert our essential wholeness, and easy when everything is going our way. Even in times of challenge, however, when tuned to wholeness, we interpret our experiences from our viewing point of wholeness. We know what we are, we appreciate the good, and we understand our experiences according to the light of truth.

The truth of wholeness is so compelling, and so amazing, it seems unfathomable that we would ever veer away from it. How easily we do, though. When we suffer a sense of human loss, when we feel unpleasant symptoms in our bodies, when we lose our jobs, when things do not go our way—we often develop spiritual amnesia. We forget our essential wholeness.

When we forget our essential wholeness, we take on an "only human" consciousness, whereby we perceive something is wrong with us. Something-wrong consciousness brings about our sense of separation from Divine Nature and our Divine Identity. Perceiving ourselves as separate, we begin to feel vulnerable to an onslaught of unwanted human conditions. We take on "only human" guilt and shame, blaming ourselves for bringing about unwanted conditions. We bargain with and beseech God to heal us of the unwanted conditions we seem to have attracted. We devolve into helpless victims crying out to a powerful superhuman for relief.

Consciousness Is Pivotal

A something-wrong consciousness is not a reality but a limited perception. A consciousness of separation is not a truth but a choice. Consciousness is pivotal.

When I married Giles in 1979, my father disowned me. Dad would not support my marriage to a man of African descent. I moved with Giles to Honolulu, where he was stationed on active duty in the US Air Force. Our children were born during that six-year assignment, after which we moved to Omaha. Throughout those years, despite letters from me and pleadings from his mother, Dad would not relent.

Others in my family, including my mother, who remained in contact with me, would tell me that Dad turned my high school graduation photo facedown on the mantel whenever he went into the living room to watch television. He hung up the telephone when I called long distance, as soon as he recognized my voice. When I returned to my hometown for my maternal grandmother's funeral, Dad walked out of the funeral home when I walked in.

The most challenging times for me, during my father's absence, were my children's births and, later, their questions. Why could they talk to their grandmother but not their grandfather? Why could we not go to Grandmom's house when we traveled to her town?

A practitioner of prayer and meditation, I persisted in my spiritual practices during nine long years of separation from my father. I made a breakthrough on the morning of my thirtieth birthday, as recorded in my journal pages on that day.

Entering meditation this morning, I invited my father into my presence. His form instantly appeared in front of me. He had aged. Wrinkles I had not known, sunken shoulders that had once stood firm, and hollow eyes on a mournful face—this was not the father of my childhood. The strong, playful daddy of my earliest memories was gone. The stern, domineering dad of my adolescence disappeared. The hard-hearted, punishing patriarch that disowned me fell away. The downcast, defeated man raised his gaze to mine, and I crumbled. Wrenching in painful sobs, I resisted what was happening in my heart. I tried to ignore the quiver of compassion stirring within me. I wanted not to love him.

Finally willing, I looked up again. The man was gone. A child was standing there instead, a vulnerable little boy, his heart shrunken in fear of being hurt. My heart over-flowed with unspeakable compassion toward him. Layers of protection I had built around my heart peeled away as I recognized, for the first time, that my father and I were the same: two souls longing for unconditional love. The child in me reached out my arms to the child in him, and I wept away the poisonous pain that had festered in my heart and mind for many years. I forgave.

The form of my father changed shape again. Now whole, transformed, lines of tension erased from his brow, my father glowed with the light of inner peace. An aura of white light surrounded his body. His arms outstretched toward me. I consciously directed Divine Love his way, wanting, needing nothing from him. I thanked him for the gift of his presence. The man who could never say to me "I love you" was letting me know not to believe his mask of disapproval. This was real, this Divine Love, this Oneness.

Years of spiritual practice had altered my perception so that I could look beyond the pain of separation from my father to the truth of our Oneness. Instead of becoming mesmerized by and attached to the painful circumstance, I was guided by and anchored in my Divine Identity. I had practiced a consciousness of wholeness, until wholeness and Oneness emerged in my experience. Even though three more years were to pass before my father and I reunited, I knew on that morning that he and I were all right.

Cultivating a Consciousness of Wholeness

We pray with wholeness in mind. We do not pray for healing. The need for healing is a thought based upon the false possibility of brokenness. Healing is the activity of recovery, repair, and restoration, correcting a consciousness that had veered away from wholeness. In other words, we heal ourselves by cultivating a consciousness of wholeness.

Shall I say it outright? GOD does not heal! GOD is wholeness. How, then, shall we pray?

Twentieth-century metaphysician Clara Palmer suggested, "When any part of your body is out of harmony, uncomfortable, or diseased, you can bless it with a living word of Truth, and it will respond." And cofounder of Unity Charles Fillmore said, "Error thoughts must be told to go, and truer thoughts must be called to take their proper place" (*Teach Us to Pray* [Unity Books: Unity Village MO, 1941], 110.) Prayer with wholeness in mind is acknowledgment of the incorruptible, uninterruptible nature of Divine Life. Prayer is asserting mental order into a chaotic consciousness. We can follow the human body's profoundly simple method for restoring order.

> Prayer with wholeness in mind is asserting mental order into a chaotic consciousness.

The human body is an aggregation of billions of cells, differentiated and yet organized and acting as one, sustaining human life. When an injury occurs, how does life in the body respond? When a bone breaks, bone cells, ligament cells, muscle cells, and nerve cells become traumatized. The alarm goes out instantly through the nervous system, broadcasting as if on the evening news *Emergency! There's trouble in our world!*

It's a good thing that the billions of uninjured cells do not respond the way billions of people respond in a world emergency. The other cells do not join the traumatized cells, behaving just like them. They do not condemn the injured leg, naming it bad or wrong. They do not attempt to cut off the leg as if the leg had failed its purpose. Good thing for us the intelligent life in the healthy cells rises up to support, sustain, and uphold life in the entire body. Amazingly, the healthy cells compensate for the injured tissue, pulling extra duty to maintain order in the body system.

Likewise, when we become aware of a nonproductive pattern of thought in our consciousness, when we suffer a disorder called doubt or fear, resulting from a human condition, prayer becomes a way of rallying healthy thought to insert order in consciousness. Healthy thought is thought attuned to truth.

An Approach to Prayer with Wholeness in Mind

Affirmative prayer during unwanted conditions shines the light of truth right into the darkness. Affirmative prayer asserts Divine Nature, recognizes our Divine Identity, and brings about realization of the highest Truth available to us at the time.

When you get sick or injured, you may go to a medical facility. There you receive support, information, and instruction, all with the aim of healing your body. If the sickness or injury is particularly serious, you may devote yourself to following a prescribed course of treatment aimed at supporting

Affirmative prayer during unwanted conditions shines the light of truth right into the darkness.

the body's capacity to express its innate wholeness. Your physician may even encourage you to devour literature about your condition and to join online chat groups to commiserate with others sharing the condition. All well and good, as long as you presume your life to be purely physical in nature.

You are coming to know that your life is *not* physical in nature. Your life does not originate in the body. The origin of your life is the One Life, One Mind—GOD. The One is whole and complete.

Therefore, you are whole and complete. When faced with physical body challenges, wouldn't it make sense also to devote time and attention toward strengthening your awareness of your essential wholeness?

In my pastoral role in ministry, I often support individuals through times of sickness. One of the ways I do this is by prescribing a spiritual practice plan that maximizes the person's focus on wholeness at a time when painful symptoms, and other people's concerns, can derail the person's attempts at wholeness consciousness.

A typical prayer prescription involves dedicated daily time for meditation, education, introspection, inspiration, and affirmation. Depending upon the person's medical regimen and daily responsibilities, I may suggest any or all of the following:

- Daily meditation: With or without instrumental background music, enter into meditation for thirty minutes twice each day. When needed, play a prerecorded guided visualization.

- Daily education: Read selected books emphasizing Divine Nature and Divine Identity. Examples are *Discover the Power Within You* by Eric Butterworth and *What Are You?* by Imelda Octavia Shanklin. Read a chapter and copy into your journal one or two sentences from the chapter to strengthen your spiritual awareness for the day.

- Daily introspection: If your journal has become your long-lost friend, reunite with it and start writing. If you are sure you will not write in a journal, find a supportive listener and start talking. Reflect upon the meaning of your life, the big picture, your sense of purpose, your Divine Identity.

- Daily inspiration: Select movies, songs, and company that uplift and inspire you, and give yourself a daily dose of one or more hours.

- Avoid shows with violence, negativity, and pathos. Turn off television and radio when not engaged in a program.

- Silence background music and reduce noise in general. This will help to quiet a busy mind.

- Choose your company. This can be challenging but is essential—avoid the company of people who "can't stand to see you so sick" and other well-meaning folks who perpetuate your image of yourself as less than whole. If you do not feel strong enough to limit your company, select someone to be your visitor gatekeeper.

- Be inspired by levity. Inspiration need not be deep and serious—select options that promote laughter and increased feelings of well-being. Read humorous books (I laughed my way through pericarditis reading Janet Evanovich's novels about the bungling bounty hunter Stephanie Plum). Watch comedies. Get outdoors for periods of time as much as possible.

- Do something out of the ordinary for you, intentionally. For example, if you tend to dress conservatively, you might borrow a friend's outrageous outfit to wear on a lunch date.

- Daily affirmation: Thirty minutes twice each day, write words of denial and affirmation that are authentic and believable right now. Don't share them aloud with a friend or just think them—for this suggestion, writing is the only option. Keep reading for some examples. Others can be found in chapter 4.

You may be thinking that you would have to alter your lifestyle and that your family would have to adapt to an intensive schedule, such as the one suggested here. You may imagine you do not have enough time every day for all this. You may not have a great deal of time or energy, especially if you are working and going through a course of medical treatment. However, consider the time you are investing in medical care. Wouldn't it seem as important to invest in spiritual care? Also, are you not now faced with an exquisite opportunity to live a ramped-up spiritual life? This is a fabulous time to alter your lifestyle in support of spiritual wholeness.

Words of Prayer with Wholeness in Mind

Here is a basic pattern for words of prayer with wholeness in mind.

1. Acknowledge divine nature.
2. Assert divine identity.
3. Deny falsehood.
4. Affirm truth.
5. Express appreciation.

Samples of prayer language follow, not to be recited verbatim but to suggest a pattern for prayer with wholeness in mind.

In Circumstances of Seasonal Allergies

It is that season again! It is the season of truth. I tell the truth to myself of the magnificent Oneness, out of which all life arises. The truth is I am one with my environment, one with trees, grasses, flowers, and everything. I am one in Divine Love, which harmonizes and unifies everything. Therefore, I cannot be ill-affected by particles in the atmosphere. I cannot be allergic to life! I stop seeking out the daily pollen count. I stop agreeing that every little sneeze confirms my fear of being harmed by allergens. I stop commiserating with others about our symptoms. I deny the possibility of being harmed by my environment, for I am Divine Love harmonizing and unifying my environment. It is that season again, the season of truth! Now I will go outdoors and play.

In Times of Financial Stress

The Earth and all of life display Divine Abundance in every way. Everywhere I turn, I see plenty. I AM Divine Abundance in the flow of giving and receiving. Divine Abundance lacks nothing and has no concept of lack. Divine Abundance I AM cannot be without all that matters to me. Divine Abundance I AM cannot suffer from financial stress. I open my eyes to look for evidence of Divine Abundance today. I notice coins on the sidewalk, kindness extended, and pleasant surprises, and I cultivate a consciousness of plenty. I express appreciation for every little good that comes my way. I bless each bill as it enters my home, and I bless each payment I make, appreciating the richness of this moment.

When Feeling Threatened by or Fearful about Physical Safety, Whether Personal or Global

In spiritual reality there is one, harmonious, unifying principle—GOD, Good. I turn my thoughts to GOD now, as I breathe harmonizing breaths. I call forth from within the unifying principle of Divine Love, of which I am made and which is my True Nature. Divine Love recognizes no threat, no enemy, and nothing to fear. I refute the energy of fear, denying fear residence in my consciousness. In the presence of Divine Love, my thoughts become clarified. I breathe easily, trusting that I am capable of responding as GOD, as Good, to anything that arises in the world. The very cells of my body are happy knowing they can relax now.

When Separated in Relationship

I recognize only One Life and One Divine Nature. My beloved and I exist within Oneness. I see that we cannot be separated in any way— not by time, distance, or emotion—and that the love we have shared cannot be lost. I remain kind in my thoughts, words, and actions. I bless my beloved's highest intentions, and I live unafraid of the future. I appreciate the countless blessings I have been given in this relationship. I bless my beloved with peace and happiness. I choose peace and happiness for myself.

In Circumstances of Cancer

My life does not spring from my body. My life springs from the one and only source of all life, which is divine. Divine Life is whole and intact. It cannot be interrupted by human circumstance or harmed by invasion. Divine Life is my life. I deny the thought of rogue cells in my body, as if something other than Divine Life could reside in me. I stand strong in spiritual authority, as one who has been sent into this darkness with a lamp. I turn on the light of truth. I am whole and complete, right now. I am whole and complete and grateful for my expanding awareness.

With practice, praying with wholeness in mind becomes the only way to pray. May you find it exhilarating to know you are not helpless against any condition and that you are empowered by deepening spiritual realization gained in prayer. Imagine how your growing spiritual consciousness can support others as you apply the principles and practices of affirmative prayer while praying with them.

Talk to Yourself

- Contemplate something about your body, aptitude, or personality that you have labeled wrong, insufficient, or incomplete. Reframe your thoughts in light of your innate wholeness.

- What have you believed about why bad things happen? Using an example from your recent history, revisit your beliefs in light of the Law of Attraction proposed in this chapter.

- Consciousness is pivotal, meaning you view your experience either from an "only human" perspective or from that of your Divine Identity. What spiritual practices do you engage in that support your remembrance of Divine Identity?

- Create a prayer prescription to follow for the next seven days.

Chapter 7

Pray with Others Affirmatively

You can be of no greater help to anyone than the measure of
truth established in your consciousness . . . Your consciousness is as infinite as God because God constitutes your consciousness, and God is infinite. All who are embraced in your
consciousness are embraced in the law of God, if you know it
and consciously remember it.

—*Joel S. Goldsmith,* The Altitude of Prayer *(1969)*

**Confidently pray with others in solitude, one-on-one, or in a
gathering of friends.**

Who do you call when the car breaks down or the washing machine overflows? You call someone who knows
about cars, or washing machines. Not necessarily a professional, either—it could be your neighbor or your sister-in-law.

When you feel afraid, consumed with sorrow, or acutely depressed, who would you call upon for true support? The pal who pats you on the back saying "How awful for you!" or the friend who sits with you silently and serenely? The one who commiserates with you or the one who reminds you of your spiritual strengths?

Have you ever felt utterly helpless when your partner, child, parent, or friend has faced a grave illness or misfortune? Besides sending flowers, dropping off meals, and calling your pastor, haven't you wished there were something you could do that would make a positive difference? There is something you can do—you can pray.

Praying with others affirmatively is a learned skill not reserved for clergy or lay leaders. Certain characteristics distinguish affirmative prayer from traditional prayer in similar circumstances.

- Do not think about prayer as a request. When asked to pray about someone's circumstance, think of the requester's intention—and name it a prayer intention. The intention, or objective, is to uphold the Divine Identity of the individual. A typical request: "Please pray for my sister, who was diagnosed with breast cancer, that she makes a full recovery." Consider the intention beneath the words—an intention for realization of Divine Life expressing as wholeness.

- Do not plead for a condition to be fixed. The work of affirmative prayer is, as Eric Butterworth taught, not to set things right but to see things rightly. For your prayer to be potent, you must see nothing needing fixing; you must see an unbroken wholeness. As long as you see sickness, you have sickness consciousness. Direct attention not to the transient condition but to the unending truth about the individual.

- Do not predict an outcome. The work of prayer is not to cast a future vision or impose your own version of an optimum conclusion. Instead, focus on the ever-present divine powers within the individual.

Praying with others affirmatively is a grand privilege and responsibility. Think about this: in your prayer with another person, in a consciousness of Oneness, you penetrate the perceived borders of a personal self and there is no *you* and *me*. You extend this realized consciousness to the other person. You know truth for her at a time that she may not realize it for herself.

Before you pray with someone, attain realized consciousness first through your daily prayer practice. If it would help you to remain centered in realized consciousness, ask a prayer partner or pastoral minister to pray with you before you pray with someone else.

Years ago I was called to the bedside of Pat G., a massage therapy client who was near death. Over ten years, she and I had become close and our relationship richly complex. She regarded me as her massage therapist and her minister. I knew her children and grandchildren, had been invited to family celebrations, and loved

In prayer with another person, in a consciousness of Oneness, there is no *you* and *me*. You extend this realized consciousness to the other person. You know truth for her at a time that she may not realize it for herself.

her deeply. I had agreed to support her and her family as she was dying and to officiate at her funeral service. The moment after I received word that her death was imminent, I telephoned a prayer partner. My intention was to be Divine Love expressing tenderness, Divine Peace exuding serenity, and Divine Strength knowing Oneness.

At the door of Pat's nursing home room, I paused, inhaled (inspired), and exhaled, observing Pat's family members encircling her bed. All hands were on her. A wave of clarity rippled through me. I felt cloaked in spiritual consciousness. I entered the room as the Light of the World, and would know Divine Purposefulness throughout the hours of Pat's transition.

Later, I cried tears of human sorrow, tempered by the memory of Pat's Divine Countenance as she exhaled her final breath. Pat's loved ones were served by my embodiment of Divine Love, Peace, and Strength so that they, too, felt capable of releasing their beloved gently and lovingly.

Whenever you are called upon to pray with someone with whom you feel especially close, understand that your spiritual clarity is the greatest support you can offer. If you cannot shake thoughts of worry, or if you cannot get out of your mind images of "his poor weakened body," you would support him best by getting prayer support for yourself before visiting.

The Five Phases of Prayer with Others

The phrase *praying with others* intentionally replaces the phrase *praying* for *others*, in consideration of the Truth of Oneness. There is only One Power, One Divine Life, Oneness. The phrase *praying with others* comes as close as we can get to unifying language.

Whenever you uphold another's intentions in prayer, whether enfolded into your daily prayer practice or at another time, follow the five phases of prayer (chapter 5) for a comprehensive, easy-to-recall pattern. In your daily prayer practice, attend to your consciousness first and then add truth ideas in support of another. When praying aloud with someone, or about them, adapt the five phases of prayer as follows:

- Relaxation: Take a few conscious, clearing breaths. Notice whether you are harboring any worry or doubt and, if so, raise your thoughts immediately to the truth that overcomes worry or doubt by silently declaring denials and affirmations.

- Concentration: Focus intently upon an affirmation essential to the circumstances. Clearly express and align with the truth. Avoid vague, weak, or untrue statements such as *All is well* or GOD *is healing you.* Speak statements of truth that uplift and strengthen. Regarding health: *Within every cell of your body, Divine Life is expressing as wholeness. You are Divine Intelligence directing Divine Ideas of strength, vitality, and purposefulness throughout your body.* Regarding grief: *You are Divine Love united with your beloved in an unending, everlasting Oneness. One in Love, One in Peace.*

- Meditation: A true state of meditation, or silence, may be unachievable during a session of abbreviated prayer. However, a moment's pause allows words of prayer to harmonize in mind and heart. Pause. Suspend thought. Be still, momentarily, knowing meditation leads to realization.

- Realization: Emphatically claim the truth, leading to actions in sync with the truth. Speak words that empower another to live into this truth. Example: *Knowing you are Divine Intelligence, your thoughts from this point forward bless your body with renewed strength, vitality, and purposefulness.* And: *You are Divine Love as you cry, laugh, celebrate, and remember Oneness in love that always has been and always will be.*

- Appreciation: Express delight in adopting a magnificent livable truth and a renewed spirit.

Whose Prayer Is It?

Does it matter whether you pray aloud with others from first, second, or third person? Practitioners in the New Thought denomination of Religious Science are taught to pray in the third person. When praying with me, for example, they might say, "Linda is guided by Divine Wisdom." When I hear a practitioner speak about me rather than to me, I feel disconnected and unmoved, although I understand practitioners speak this way so as not to presume a consciousness for someone else.

Others pray in second person. I may pray in second person when I sense someone appears to be struggling with acceptance of her Divine Identity. I might look into her eyes and say, directly, "I know who you are. You are Divine Wisdom." Praying in second person can effectively catapult a person into a fresh awareness of her True Nature, or ineffectively, it can appear an attempt at convincing a person to believe something she does not yet believe about herself.

Praying in first person is also an option. In first person language, you connect with the person's intention by speaking as the person—suggesting he listen with the idea that your words represent his own Divine Wisdom speaking. "I AM Divine Wisdom expressing . . ." and continue adopting the person's prayer intention.

Your preference for speaking in first, second, or third person in prayer with others is just that—your preference. Understand your reasoning for speaking as you do, and develop the manner of speaking most powerful, and most effective, for you and for that other person.

Praying Aloud in a Gathering

Most people feel relieved if a minister or someone trained in prayer is present to offer prayers at the start and end of a gathering. Rarely will anyone else volunteer for this seemingly daunting challenge of giving words to our shared spiritual experience. Imagine a community where you could turn to anyone nearby, asking for prayer support and being able to trust words will flow from a rising consciousness of Divine Identity. Imagine returning the favor too.

I believe people's reluctance to lead prayer stems from a reparable issue. We don't feel confident because we are not practiced at constructing potent statements of Truth. Practice, then. This will benefit you and everyone you lead in prayer.

When you become the prayer leader, it may help for you to have in mind a pattern similar to the pattern of your daily prayer practice. The following pattern uses the five phases of prayer with variations applicable to groups.

1. Relaxation: The intention in relaxation is to cast off sluggishness and stress and become conscious of being in a spiritualized atmosphere. Invite everyone to stretch (especially helpful when meeting in evening hours), breathe deeply, and send relaxation messages to her and his body and brain. Slow down. Savor the moment.

2. Concentration: This phase of prayer sometimes is labeled invocation. Although the word *invocation* commonly means to call upon a deity, it literally means to call forth from within. This is precisely what we aim for in the concentration phase of prayer. Acknowledge the broadest truth you know and feel inspired to speak. Speak of Divine Nature, Oneness, Divine Love, or any Divine Quality. Simply state the truth in words you have heard before or in your own style. For example, you could restate a frequently heard affirmation in Unity communities: "There is only One Presence and One Power, GOD, Good."

3. Meditation: As noted elsewhere, unless the group is gathering with the intention of meditating as one, a moment of silent reflection gives everyone an opportunity to internalize the words expressed by the prayer leader. Ideally, a moment of silence promotes realization thinking.

4. Realization: Emphatically claim the truth arising from this prayer time, directing the group's attention toward

collective actions based upon the truth. The collective realization can be expressed in an affirmation, such as, *In all our interactions today, we are One Mind expressing as Wisdom, Order, and Joy.* Alternatively, invite everyone to share individual realizations. Adding other voices in realization increases attendees' buy-in, as it expands communal spiritual vitality.

5. Appreciation: Avoid unthinking statements directed at a superhuman deity, such as "Thank you for bringing us together" or "Thank you for this opportunity to come together." Instead, try "We enjoy the harmony of our shared intention. We celebrate our joint passion and dedication to our work (study, service). Amen (we commit to this way of being)."

At the close of a gathering, the group prayer may entirely consist of expressions of appreciation. If you are leading a closing prayer, relate back to the intentions and realizations at the start of the gathering and express appreciation for their fulfillment. Avoid words of appreciation limited to the group's material agenda, such as "we appreciate everyone's efforts toward completion of our project." Reach for appreciation of the group's Divine Qualities expressed in this gathering. Invite others to share a word or phrase of appreciation, when appropriate.

Many groups include personal prayer intentions within closing prayer, which often increase feelings of mutual support and interconnectedness. Rather than responding to each stated prayer intention, speak a single potent affirmation of confidence in everyone's Divine Identity. For example: *We uphold one another's Divine Identity and spiritual capacities, confident that as we realize truth, we breathe truth into these prayer intentions and into all our hearts' desires.*

Prayer Partnership

During the past eleven years, I have kept a sacred appointment nearly every Tuesday morning with my prayer partner. We meet over the telephone with the sole intention of praying together. We take turns briefly identifying our prayer intentions, and then one follows the lead of the other, who prays aloud. We agree that our purpose is prayer, not counseling or chitchat, and we conclude within twenty minutes. Over the years we have divulged much about ourselves to each other. We have come to know and respect each other. Even so, we carefully do not interfere in each other's concerns. Occasionally, with the partner's agreement, one of us might share an insight arising about the partner's intention or ask for feedback about her own intention. Our persistence in this prayer partnership testifies to the value of shared prayer, which supports our living as the Light of the World.

We uphold one another's Divine Identity and spiritual capacities, confident that as we realize truth, we breathe truth into our prayer intentions and into all our hearts' desires.

Prayer partnerships need not be limited to two. A small group of dedicated prayer partners can boost individual consciousness—"where two or three are gathered in my name, *I* am there among them" (Matthew 18:20). A select group might assemble in support of a friend experiencing challenging circumstances. A group might be drawn together over the same or similar conditions, such as job searching or recuperating from cancer treatment. A group might form after studying prayer together in a class. However your prayer group forms, consider these recommendations:

- Assemble a group of two to six participants, obtaining everyone's agreement to full participation. Consider the group closed to others, not in an attitude of exclusivity but to maintain an environment in which participants can share sincerely and safely.

- Agree about meeting time, length, location, and frequency. If your group uses the following affirmative shared prayer format, allow twenty to thirty minutes for a group of six. Schedule weekly meetings.

- Agree about a start and end date. Agree to a first period of six weeks, and then renegotiate as the end date nears.

- Agree about mutual expectations concerning confidentiality, extraneous conversation, absenteeism, and other matters of trust and comfort.

- Designate one person the leader at the start of each session. The leader senses when it is time to proceed to the next segment and names the next segment aloud.

Affirmative Shared Prayer

Although five phases of prayer are taught in earlier chapters, affirmative shared prayer consists of eight segments. In addition to the five phases, affirmative shared prayer provides group practice in naming prayer intentions and using the tools of denial and affirmation. The eight segments of affirmative shared prayer are

1. relaxation

2. concentration

3. meditation

4. intention

5. denial

6. affirmation/realization

7. commitment

8. appreciation

A pattern of language and instruction follows for each of the eight segments. To begin, you might light a candle representing Divine Nature and your unity of purpose in prayer.

1. Relaxation
[Speak together] *"I breathe consciously, releasing physical and mental tension. I turn my attention to the Divine Nature of the present moment. I relax and open to Oneness."*

The title *Divine Nature* in this prayer sequence is one way to speak of GOD without connoting a superhuman deity. *Divine Nature* refers to infinite, immutable, and inexhaustible spiritual reality. You may prefer another title more fitting to the group's faith tradition or shared vernacular.

Conscious relaxation clears the space, literally and energetically. Everyone's conscious relaxation contributes to the spiritualized environment in which you open to Oneness. After reciting the relaxation affirmation in unison, pause for a full minute to give all a chance to practice conscious relaxation.

2. Concentration

[Speaking together] *"There is only One Divine Nature, infinite, immutable, and inexhaustible. Everything and everyone derives its identity from One Divine Nature. Divine Nature is my nature. I AM Divine."*

In unison, recite the statement of concentration as a means of turning your thoughts to this most expansive spiritual truth. Pausing, reflect upon the magnificence of this truth—the meaning of infinite, immutable, and inexhaustible pointing to your unlimited divine potential. Hold the thought *Divine Nature is my nature. I AM divine*, so that it fills your consciousness.

3. Meditation

Be still and know that I AM divine.

Pause for a full minute or longer, stilling thoughts and resting in the pervasive Divine Nature of this moment.

4. Intention

[Speaking individually] *"I AM divine. My prayer intention is . . ."*

In turn, each participant vocalizes a prayer intention. A prayer intention is a statement of desired consciousness in the midst of a circumstance. Frame your prayer intention by acknowledging I AM divine. Now, name how you intend to express Divine Nature.

Instead of "My prayer request is for a friend who just got laid off from her job," you might say *"My prayer intention is to be Divine*

Abundance upholding my friend as she moves into a bright future." Or *"My prayer intention is for my friend's realization of her Divine Power of Abundance."*

Instead of "My prayer request is for healing of shingles," you might say *"My prayer intention is to stand strong in Divine Wholeness while my body recovers its natural health and vitality."*

Divine Nature expresses as powers or capacities intrinsic to our True Nature. Whatever is true of Divine Nature may be claimed and expressed by us, intentionally. We claim and express these Divine Powers to identify with Divine Nature, which prompts our living of these Divine Capacities in the midst of all circumstances. Our greatest potential is to become the Light of the World, revealing Divine Nature wherever we are.

A prayer intention is always for what you want to be rather than for a resolution or preferred outcome. Actually, you already are All That Is; your prayer intention is to realize it. As each person speaks in turn, everyone else listens, reflecting back spiritual support. In the subsequent segments of affirmative shared prayer, use the tools of denial and affirmation to disclaim your false identity and assert your Divine Identity.

5. Denial

[Speaking together] *"I release all mistaken judgments and untrue assumptions about myself, others, and my prayer intention. I deny false ideas any control over my consciousness."*

As spiritual realization begins to dawn, very often our "only human" sense of self argues against our Divine Identity. Practicing denial raises our awareness of our false ideas, for the purpose of casting them out of our consciousness. Pause after reciting the statement of denial in unison. Notice or recall thoughts you have harbored in disharmony with your prayer intention. Silently deny their truthfulness and their influence over you.

6. Affirmation/Realization
[Speaking individually] *"I claim the Divine Power of . . . I AM the Divine Power of . . ."*

Contemplate one or more aspects of Divine Nature that, when you claim and embody them, transform the way you respond to the situation identified earlier in this prayer session. Claim the Divine Capacities necessary for you to live your prayer intention.

Referring back to the prayer intention to be Divine Abundance, an affirmation might be stated this way: *"I claim the Divine Power of Abundance. I AM Divine Abundance celebrating an outpouring of opportunities for my friend's success and prosperity. I radiate Divine Abundance in all my encounters with my friend, knowing my friend's True Nature also is abundance."*

As each in turn voices his and her affirmation, everyone else listens in agreement and support.

7. Commitment
[Speaking individually] *"To practice living as the Divine Power of . . . , I promise within the next twenty-four hours to . . ."* [Identify a specific action demonstrating your Divine Power in fulfillment of your prayer intention].

A potent way of establishing spiritual realization is to demonstrate it by meaningful action. Actually, truth is never realized unless it is lived. Consider some possible actions that would reveal the Divine Power you have chosen to express. An effective action is clear, specific, and noticeable. When you have completed this action, you will know you have fulfilled your commitment.

Here are some examples for demonstrating Divine Abundance:

To practice living as the Divine Power of Abundance, I promise within the next twenty-four hours to interview my friend, inviting her to talk about her strengths, skills, talents, and interests. I will ask her about her favorite activities in childhood, in school, and in work. I will listen for and sense her passions, reflecting these back to her. I will celebrate her magnificent, abundant Divine Qualities.

I will light a candle representing my friend's Divine Nature and list all the Divine Qualities about her that come to mind. I will place this list next to the candle and refer to it whenever I notice my thoughts turning to worry about her well-being.

Avoid nonspecific promises such as "I will think positive thoughts about my friend." As each person promises an action, others listen in agreement and support. If anyone seems to be struggling in this segment, at that person's request, the group may offer ideas. Everyone wants to live in spiritual realization. Everyone wants to close this session knowing how to fulfill prayer intention.

8. Appreciation

[Speaking together] *"In Oneness, we bless, appreciate, and celebrate our Divine Nature. We uphold one another's intentions. We exude appreciation, for we are truly blessed. Amen."*

Conscious appreciation magnifies our blessings. We *are* truly blessed by one another's willingness to be the Light of the World.

Talk to Yourself

- Reflect upon a time you felt concern enough for a loved one that you prayed with that person. Was your prayer a prayer of faith or a prayer of desperation? Would you pray differently today? What would be different?

- In prayer with others, we are not declaring a desired outcome; instead, we are expressing words of confidence in the perfect Divine Life of another, calling that life into expression. Talk about the difference between saying, "I see this illness healed" and, "Divine Life is flowing in and through this person."

- Some people believe you must ask a person's permission before holding him in prayer, as if your prayer could interfere with his will. Based upon what you know and are learning, why is this concern unnecessary?

- In advance of a meeting with others, reflect upon the meeting intentions and the attendees' Divine Qualities. Practice statements of invocation (bringing to mind Divine Qualities), affirmation, and appreciation. Your preparation may lead you to volunteer as prayer leader, but it will do much more: your preparation will carry your spiritual consciousness into the meeting.

Affirmative Shared Prayer: Removable Guide

1. Relaxation

   [Speaking together] *"I breathe consciously, releasing physical and mental tension. I turn my attention to the Divine Nature of the present moment. I relax and open to Oneness."*

2. Concentration

   [Speaking together] *"There is only One Divine Nature, infinite, immutable, and inexhaustible. Everything and everyone derives its identity from One Divine Nature. Divine Nature is my nature. I AM Divine."*

3. Meditation

   Be still and know that I AM *Divine.* Pause for a full minute or longer, stilling thoughts and resting in the pervasive Divine Nature of this moment.

4. Intention

   [Speaking individually] *"I AM divine. My prayer intention is . . ."*

5. Denial

   [Speaking together] *"I release all mistaken judgments and untrue assumptions about myself, others, and my prayer intention. I deny false ideas any control over my consciousness."*

6. Affirmation/Realization

   [Speaking individually] *"I claim the Divine Power of . . . I AM the Divine Power of . . ."*

7. Commitment

   [Speaking individually] *"To practice living as the Divine Power of . . . , I promise within the next twenty-four hours to . . ."* [Identify a specific action demonstrating your Divine Power in fulfillment of your prayer intention.]

8. Appreciation

   [Speaking together] *"In Oneness, we bless, appreciate, and celebrate our Divine Nature. We uphold one another's intentions. We exude appreciation, for we are truly blessed. Amen."*

About the Author

Winner of *The 2011 Best Spiritual Author* competition, Linda Martella-Whitsett is an inspiring, respected Unity minister and spiritual teacher. Linda's message about our Divine Identity inspires people across cultures and faith traditions to meet life's circumstances with spiritual maturity. Linda is the senior minister at Unity Church of San Antonio and a mentor for emerging leaders in New Thought. Visit her online at *www.ur-divine.com* or *www.lindamartella-whitsett.com.*

Hampton Roads Publishing Company

... for the evolving human spirit

Hampton Roads Publishing Company publishes books on a variety of subjects, including spirituality, health, and other related topics.

For a copy of our latest trade catalog, call (978) 465-0504 or visit our distributor's website at *www.redwheelweiser.com.*